Bible Time
for Active Kids

Malinda Fugate

Bible Time for Active Kids

Copyright © 2018 Malinda Fugate
Original Cover Art: Amanda Ruth Art
Original Illustrations: John Snyder

All rights reserved.

Scriptures taken from the Holy Bible, New International Version®, NIV®. Copyright © 1973, 1978, 1984, 2011 by Biblica, Inc.™ Used by permission of Zondervan. All rights reserved worldwide. www.zondervan.com The "NIV" and "New International Version" are trademarks registered in the United States Patent and Trademark Office by Biblica, Inc.™

ISBN: 1987414314
ISBN-13: 978-1987414318

Bible Time for Active Kids

To all the Faith Crusaders, who teach me every week.

Bible Time for Active Kids

TABLE OF CONTENTS

Bible Time For Active Kids Family Challenge 7
God Creates The World 14
The Temptation Of Adam And Eve 16
Tower Of Babel 19
Noah And The Ark 21
Abram And Sarai Take A Trip 24
God's Promise To Abraham 27
Jacob And Esau 30
Joseph And His Brothers 33
Joseph Forgives 36
Baby Moses 39
Moses And The Burning Bush 41
Moses And Pharaoh 44
The Red Sea 46
Israelites In The Wilderness 49
Joshua, Caleb, And The Spies 51
Gideon 54
Samson 57
Ruth 60
Samuel Hears God 62
Samuel Appoints David 65
David The Shepherd 68
David And Goliath 70
Rebuilding The Temple 73
Esther 75
Job 77
Psalm 19 79
Psalm 34 81
Psalm 47 83
Psalm 139 85
Proverbs- Friends 88
Proverbs- Ants 90
Jonah And The Big Fish 92
John The Baptist 95
Jesus Is Born 97
Boy Jesus In Temple 100
Parable Of The Sower 103
Parable Of Good Samaritan 106
Kids In The Bible 109

Love Your Enemies 111
Jesus The Carpenter 113
Fishing For People 115
Zacchaeus 118
Jesus Heals The Blind 120
Mary And Martha 122
Parable Of The Talents 124
Jesus Raises Lazarus 127
Jesus And The Tax Collector 129
The Wise Man And The Foolish Man 131
Jesus Heals A Deaf Man 133
The Lord's Prayer 135
Flowers And Sparrows 137
Triumphal Entry 139
Jesus Dies On The Cross 141
Christ Is Risen! 144
The First Church 147
Saul's Conversion 150
Dorcas 152
Paul's Letters 154
Paul's Journey 157
Running The Race 159
What Is Sin? 161
Draw Close To God 163
Jesus Will Come Again 165
Are You A Writer Today? 168
Cardboard Box 170
Bible Time For A Friend 172
Serving God 175
Conclusion 177

Bible Time for Active Kids is a devotional Bible study just for you. It's a way we can study God's word when it feels like we have lots of energy and sitting still is difficult. Most chapters are designed for kids to do on their own, but some days give you a chance to spend time together with God and your family or friends.

To begin, take the Bible Time for Active Kids family challenge! Make a little bit of time to do each mini Bible study as a family. There will always be a verse to learn and an activity that makes the lesson easy to understand. Find what works best for your family and stick with it. Maybe your best time is in the afternoon, or the evening before bed. You might start a Bible Time journal to write down the answers to questions- then look back to see what you've learned later in the year. Maybe it's better to answer the questions out loud and then keep the memory verse on the fridge or in the car as a reminder. Be creative and have fun- there is joy in spending time with the Lord!

Here we go!

Day 1:

When we become Christians, we are completely changed.

Read together: 2 Corinthians 5:17

This means our lives are different after Jesus is in our hearts. What are some differences in the day-to-day lives of Christians and non-believers?

Sometimes, many things in life keep us busy. What things keep your family busy during the week?

Look up this verse: Mark 12:30

How can your family remember to love Jesus this week?

Pray about it: Thank God for being with us every day. Ask Him to help you love Him with all your mind, heart, and strength.

Family time!

Make a chart similar to the one on the next page and hang it somewhere everyone can see and reach it. Include each member of the family, and list different ways to love and serve God through our actions. Some examples could be "read the Bible," "pray as a family," "help someone," "have a kind attitude," or "learn this week's memory verse." Encourage each other by awarding a sticker or drawing a star when each person is "caught" loving God this week!

	Pray together	Read the Bible	Help Someone	Memory Verse
Dad				
Mom				
Sister				
Brother				

Day 2:

Read together: Exodus 3

Think about a jigsaw puzzle. You don't complete an entire puzzle at once, but you do it piece by piece. You examine each part and focus on one area at a time. The edge pieces create the frame and then similar colors fit together. The picture on the box gives you a reference, showing you the final goal. God works like that, too. He doesn't give us a big map of our future. Instead, we get step-by-step instructions. Sometimes He shows us the big picture, and other times just enough so we know what to do with the pieces in our hand.

If God showed Moses the big picture, Moses never would have known how to go from baby-sitting sheep in the wilderness to leading a nation to the Promised Land. Yet, his shepherd skills trained him to baby-sit the Israelite "sheep" wandering the desert all those years. God's perfect method guided Moses from a burning bush to negotiating with Pharaoh, and all the way to the revealing of His glory.

Look up this verse: Proverbs 3:5-6

Pray about it: Ask God for guidance and wisdom each day- and maybe even to see the divine "big picture" of the plans and purposes for each member of your family.

Family time!
Find a jigsaw puzzle and work on it together. Talk about how God shows us His plan piece-by-piece.

Day 3:

Read together: Matthew 7:16-20

How do you know if a tree is an apple tree? (Because it grows apples!) What about an orange tree? A grape vine? How do we tell if a plant is a weed?

Just like we know when a plant is good or bad, the Bible says you can tell what people are like by their "fruits"- what kinds of things grow from their hearts. Do you know people who smile a lot? They have happy hearts. What about people who always help others? Or those who are often angry? What other "fruits" can you think of?

When we have God in our hearts, we grow "fruit of the Spirit." These are gifts we get from the Holy Spirit. The more time we spend with God, the more the fruit of the spirit grows!

Look up this verse: Galatians 5:22
List each of the fruits of the Spirit. Which of these can you see in your family?

Pray about it: Thank God for the fruits of the Spirit in our lives, and ask that we show more of them each day.

Family time!
As a family, make a fruit salad! You can also place fruit on skewers and make colorful kebabs. Use one real fruit for each "fruit of the spirit" (for example, maybe strawberries represent love, oranges represent joy, etc.). See who can name all of the spiritual "fruits" from memory!

Day 4:

Read together: 1 Samuel 17:1-50 or the story of David and Goliath in a children's Bible

How do you think David felt when he fought Goliath?
Did his family and friends help him?
Have you ever felt like David? When?

We might not fight giant people, but sometimes we have "giants" of our own to battle. They can be challenges like tough tests at school or a big project at work. What are some "giants" that each person in your family faces?

Some of these things just seem too big or impossible to handle. But did David fight Goliath on his own? What was David's secret to success?

Look up this verse: Matthew 17:20
What did Jesus say someone needed to have to move mountains?
How can you fight your "giants" together with God?

Pray about it: Thank God for helping us face the giants in our lives and ask Him to keep us strong when we battle obstacles and challenges.

Family time!
Tell the story of David and Goliath by acting it out. Be creative! You can dress in costumes, draw a picture, use puppets or toys, or anything your imagination decides.

Day 5:

Read together: Philemon 9-16

The name "Onesimus" means "useful." This story doesn't give us many details, but how do you think Onesimus could have been useful to Paul?

Identity means "who you are." Onesimus probably thought he was just a slave, but Paul calls him a "son" and later a "brother." What is your identity? Son? Daughter? Sister? Father? Can it be more than one thing? Who do you think God says you are?

Look up this verse: John 15:15
Help each other memorize this verse this week! Quiz each other, say it together, or make it fun!

Pray about it: Pray together as a family, thanking God for loving us and showing us how precious we are to Him.

Family time!
We learned that the name "Onesimus" means "useful," but what does your name mean? Use a baby name book or internet resources to discover the meaning of each family member's name. Parents, share the reasons why you chose your children's names.

Bible Time for Active Kids

Spend some one-on-one time with God who loves you. Do a page a day, once a week, or even every few days. It's up to you! Read the scripture at the beginning of each section from your Bible- even a children's Bible that tells the story is great! It's important for us to spend as much time in God's word as possible. At the end of each Bible Time, there's space to write your thoughts. You can write a prayer, note something new you learned, or record which activities you did. At the end, you'll be able to look back on all your time with the Lord. Are you ready? Let's start at the beginning…

God Creates the World

The Scripture: Genesis 1-2

Think about it:
God created our whole world in a week! He started with light and darkness, then made everything from land and sea to animals and people. How amazing! Make sure to read this spectacular story in the Bible. It's so good, you won't want to miss it.

God did an incredible thing by making an entire universe out of absolutely nothing. That's impossible for any person to do. We have to start with something that already exists if we want to make anything.

But, God did make us in His image, and God is an expert creator. He gave us the ability to be creative and use our imaginations, too. We can be creative in many ways- being artistic, inventing things, designing things, dreaming new ideas and more. How do you like to be creative?

Using our God-given creative talents is one way to give praise and worship to the Lord. How can you practice creating this week? Can you share it with others? How will you bless God with your creativity?

Look up this memory verse and say it out loud: Genesis 1:1
"In the beginning, God created the heavens and the earth."

Pray about it: Thank God for His incredible creation! Ask Him to be with you as you create something.

Active time!

Create something (I bet you saw that coming)! Decide what kind of project best uses your unique talents. Will you draw or paint? Build something like a fort or use Lego bricks? Maybe you're creative in the kitchen or the garden. Pick a project, give it your best effort, and enjoy time with God while using the creative ability He gave you!

Bonus fun: Think about what the Garden of Eden was like. Then, take a walk outside and collect some nature items that you can use to decorate a picture frame.

My Time With God:

The Temptation of Adam and Eve

The Scripture: Genesis 2:4-3:24

Think about it:
Adam and Eve were very happy living in the beautiful Garden of Eden. God gave them everything they needed with a few simple rules to keep them healthy and happy. But one day, something went wrong.

Do you know the word "temptation"? Have you ever heard someone say, "Oh, that's tempting"?

Temptation is the opportunity to do something that is wrong or against God's Word. God told Adam and Eve that they could eat fruit from any tree they wanted, but they only had to stay away from one specific tree in the middle of Garden of Eden. Along came the devil disguised as a snake to tell them to eat the fruit anyway, even though God said no. That was temptation. Adam and Eve had a choice, and they chose to listen to the snake instead of listening to God. They ate the fruit from the special tree that God told them not to touch. Because they broke the rules, they were no longer allowed to live in the beautiful garden.

Our temptation doesn't come from talking animals, but we have to make the choice to follow God's Word every day. We might be tempted to cheat on a test if we don't know the answers, or to lie to our parents to stay out of trouble. But, even when it's hard, we need to listen to God and ignore anything that is not His truth.

Resisting temptation is hard, but God helps us. All we have to do is ask Him, and He will give us the strength to make the right choice! Meanwhile, the consequences of giving into temptation are usually even more difficult. For example, cheating on a test or lying to parents will end in bigger trouble than making the right choice in the first place. What do you think would've happened to Adam and Eve if they listened to God instead of the snake?

What tempts you? What choices are hard for you to make? How will you ask God to help you resist temptation?

Look up this memory verse and say it out loud: 1 Corinthians 10:13
"And God is faithful; He will not let you be tempted beyond what you can bear. But when you are tempted, He will also provide a way out so that you can endure it."

Pray about it: Thank God for helping you resist temptation. Ask Him to be with you as you make good choices. Also, ask Him to help you see His truth clearly.

Active time!
Practice resisting temptation. Choose something you really enjoy, like watching television, playing on a smartphone, or eating your favorite food. Make a decision not to do that thing for a whole week! You might be tempted to give up and do it anyway, but try to resist. When we practice resisting temptation, it helps make us stronger when the big stuff comes around.

Bonus fun: Make cardboard figures of Adam, Eve, and the snake. Attach each of them to a craft stick. Place them in a garden or potted plant to remind you of the story and resisting temptation.

My Time With God:

Tower of Babel

The Scripture: Genesis 11:1-9

Think about it:

Normally, teamwork is a good thing. What are some good times to work together as a group?

The ancient people in Shinar were really good at teamwork. Their plan to build a tall tower was working nicely! There was just one problem....

The people of Shinar had a reason to build the tallest tower. It wasn't because they liked fancy buildings or thought teamwork was fun. They "wanted to make a name for themselves". This means they didn't care about anything but being famous. They had too much pride in themselves, which leaves no time or energy to worship God.

The Lord saw that this wasn't a good plan. So He divided the people by giving them different languages. Can you imagine the confusion? What do you think happened at the moment that God changed their speech? Without being able to talk to each other, the people could not continue to build their tall tower.

When we are working together with God, He makes all things possible. But when we only care about ourselves, we won't get very far. What dreams are most important to you? Where does God fit into your dreams and plans?

Look up this memory verse and say it out loud: Matthew 19:26 "Jesus looked at [the disciples] and said, "With man this is impossible, but with God all things are possible."

Pray about it: Thank God for helping us work together. Ask Him to be in all your dreams and plans, so that everything you do brings glory to Him.

Active time!
Use a book, app, or website to learn a new language! Many resources are available to help you. Then, be creative and invent your own language to share with a sibling or a friend.

Bonus fun: Build a tall tower out of blocks, boxes, pillows, or anything else you find. How tall can you reach?

<u>My Time With God:</u>

Noah and the Ark

The Scripture: Genesis 6:9-9:17

Think about it:

There came a time when all the people on earth turned away from God. In all the world, there was one family who obeyed God. Noah was a good, righteous man, and so was his family. One day, God told Noah that He was going to destroy the earth with a flood. However, Noah and his family would be safe. God told Noah to build a really big boat called an ark. Then, He brought two of each kind of animal to the ark so they would be safe when it started to flood. When it was time, God shut the door to the big boat and it began to rain. It kept raining for 40 days and 40 nights, until the whole world was covered with water.

This familiar story sounds really fun when we think of Noah's floating zoo. It was the first jungle cruise! Imagine hanging out with all the animals. What would you do if you could spend a day with an elephant? What would you say to a giraffe? Could you feed a porcupine?

Now think about spending over a month on a big wooden boat with only your family and a BUNCH of wild animals. Animals that ALL have to be fed every day... Animals that make smelly messes... And nothing but water as far as the eye could see... What would THAT be like?

After weeks and weeks of hard work while trapped on a boat, it would be easy for Noah to forget that God was in control of the situation. But Noah stayed faithful to God. When it was time, Noah sent out birds to look for dry land. When they finally landed on a mountain top, everyone left the ark. The first thing Noah and his family did was worship God. God wanted to make sure Noah always remembered His promise to never flood the earth again, so He made a rainbow in the sky. And God put many rainbows in the sky for years after, just to remind Noah- and all the people- about that promise.

God makes promises to you, too. He promised to never leave you and to always take care of you. Can you think of any other promises God has made? He sent the rainbow to you, too. Every time you see a rainbow, remember God's promises!

Look up this memory verse and say it out loud: Hebrews 10:23 "God can be trusted to keep his promise."

Pray about it: Thank God for His faithful promises. Ask Him to help you trust Him during the hardest challenges.

Active time!
Spend time with animals! If you have a pet, take extra time today to play with him or her. You can also volunteer at an animal

shelter or offer to walk your neighbor's dog. You might even ask a parent to visit a pet store or a zoo.

Bonus fun: Have you ever made a rainbow? Research how rainbows are made, then use a prism, glass of water, or even a CD to put your own rainbow on a wall.

My Time With God:

Abram and Sarai Take a Trip

The Scripture: Genesis 12:1-4a

Think about it:
There was a man named Abram who loved God. One day, God told Abram to leave his country and his family and travel to new places. He said He would bless Abram and all of the future generations of his family. So Abram obeyed God. He gathered his family and they followed God's directions.

This short beginning to the story of Abram (who became Abraham) is packed full of things for us, too. First, it gives a good example of how to respond to God's instruction. Just like Abram and Sarai (God later changed her name to Sarah), we should be obedient when we hear from Him. Though God doesn't often speak to us in a loud, booming voice, we can find His instructions clearly written in the Bible.

Can you think of a few of God's directions? What are they telling us to do?

Other important things in this story are the promises that God gave Abram and Sarai. Sometimes, blessings come right after following God's instructions. God wants to do good things in our lives, and His commands are the directions to get to those good things.

Can you think of any of God's other promises in the Bible? How is God blessing you and your family?

Finally, we often remember Abram and Sarai as an example of acting with faith. Faith means believing and trusting God, even if you can't see what will happen next. Abram and Sarai's journey took them to unknown places. Do you think they might have been a little scared to go? But they still began to travel, trusting that God's directions were the best way.

Is there anything you feel like God is telling you to do that needs some faith?

Look up this memory verse and say it out loud: Galatians 3:7 "Understand, then, that those who have faith are children of Abraham."

Pray about it: Thank God for His instructions and blessings. Ask Him to show you where to go this week.

Active time!
Is your family going on a trip soon? Help plan your route on a map and make a list of things to do while you are away! If you don't have a trip coming up, imagine you can go anywhere and make plans for the excursion in as much detail as possible. Who knows, maybe you'll make that journey in the future!

Bonus fun: Go on a journey that God leads! Take a "prayer walk" around your neighborhood. Pray for your neighbors and any community issues. Ask God to give you direction as you walk. Before you go, talk to a parent or bring them along for safety.

My Time With God:

God's Promise to Abraham

The Scripture: Genesis 15:1-7

Just like God made a promise to Noah, He also made a promise to Abraham. And just like God gave Noah a reminder, He gave Abraham a reminder of his promise, too. But instead of a rainbow, the symbol of Abraham's promise was in the stars.

One night, God told Abraham that he would have a son. Then He said that Abraham would have so many descendants that they'd be as many as the stars in the sky. (Descendants means children, grandchildren, great-grandchildren, and all the family that comes along after you.) God also promised to give Abraham and his descendants a land of their very own.

When God promises something, it's sometimes easy and exciting to believe it right away! But, it can also be difficult to patiently wait for God to take time to complete His work. We like things to happen quickly- especially good things! But God knows more than we do, and has every detail covered. It might take a little longer to see His promise than we think it should.

God knows that it's hard for us to wait. We might start to doubt His promises and think they're never going to happen! Abraham and Sarah had to wait a long time before they saw God's promise and had their own son. It took even longer for their son to grow up and start his own family. And Abraham could never live long enough to see the complete promise of many generations of his descendants! Abraham had to trust God to keep the promise. Every time Abraham looked up at the stars, he could remember His promise and believe it. Do you think that made it a little easier to wait?

Have you waited a long time for a promise? What helped you keep believing the promise would be true?

Look up this memory verse and say it out loud: Hebrews 10:23 "Let us hold firmly to the hope we claim to have. The God who promised is faithful."

Pray about it: Thank God for His promises. Ask Him to help you remember those promises, even if they take a long time.

Active time!
Look at the night sky and go star-gazing! Take a blanket to the backyard and look up at the night sky. You can use an app like "Sky Map" or a book about constellations to try to identify the patterns of the stars. Find the moon, your favorite constellation, and some planets. You might even see a shooting star!

Bonus fun: God gave another symbol of His promise when He changed Abram's name to Abraham and Sarai's name to Sarah. Think about your name. What does it mean?

Now think about something God promised you. If you had a new name to remember that promise, what would it be? Use a baby name book or website (such as www.behindthename.com) to look up a name by its meaning, and imagine what name God might give you to remember His promises. For example, the name "Manuel" means "God with us" and is a reminder that God will never leave you. Also, "Victoria" means "victory", and could remind you that God promised to be victorious over the devil. What other names can you find?

<u>My Time With God:</u>

Jacob and Esau

The Scripture: Genesis 25:19–34, 27:1-43

Do you always get along with your brother or sister? Sometimes it's easy to love our siblings, but sometimes it can be a challenge! Tell your sibling about the best time you had together. Then tell each other about a time when you fought with each other. Which memories are better? Can you learn anything from the sad memories?

Sometimes, our conflicts can get out of hand. That's what happened to Esau and Jacob in this story. Even though they were twin brothers, Esau and Jacob were very different from each other. They were not good friends.

They were born on the same day, but Esau came right before Jacob. That meant that he was the oldest and would get their father's blessing. But Jacob wanted the blessing, too. One day, Esau was out hunting and Jacob was home. He made a delicious stew so it was ready as soon as Esau returned. Esau was very hungry and thought the stew smelled delicious! But Jacob would only give him food if he promised to give their father's blessing to Jacob. Esau was so hungry that he said yes! He gave away something very special and important for a cup of soup.

When we let our hurt and frustration grow, we sometimes say and do things we regret later. How do you think Jacob and Esau felt after all the stew was gone and the deal was complete?

When they grew up, their father still wanted to give Esau the blessing, So Jacob made a sneaky plan with their mother. When Esau was out hunting, Jacob dressed in a disguise. Then he went in to see their father, who was blind and couldn't see Jacob clearly. Jacob pretended to be Esau and got the blessing! What a mean trick!

If you could give Esau and Jacob any advice, what would it be? Check out the memory verse for instructions from God.

Look up this memory verse and say it out loud: Ephesians 4:2 "Be completely humble and gentle; be patient, bearing with one another in love."

Pray about it: Thank God for giving us brothers and sisters (or even cousins or friends who are like siblings). Ask God to help you love each other.

Active time!
You can make soup to share, but you don't have to do it like Jacob. Instead of tricking your family, make a delicious stew with love. You can look for a recipe in a cookbook or ask a parent to help you make a favorite kind of soup. Or, you can even warm up ready-made soup from a box or can!

Bonus fun: Make a disguise! You can use old clothes and hats, or pull out your craft supplies to create a mysterious mask. Try changing your voice or moving in different ways to make your transformation complete. Then, tell the story of Jacob and Esau to someone else as your new character.

My Time With God:

Joseph and His Brothers

The Scripture: Genesis 37:1–4, 12–28

Joseph came from a big family. He had 11 brothers! But out of all 12 kids, Joseph was their dad's favorite. He loved Joseph so much that he gave him a special present- a beautiful robe.

This made the other brothers mad and jealous of Joseph. One day, Joseph told his brothers about a dream he had about the sun, moon, and stars. The dream meant that all the family would bow down to him. This made the brothers even angrier!

Sometimes our family is like Joseph's family. We don't always get along. Sometimes we disagree or even fight. But we never stop loving each other! Joseph's father, Jacob, gave him a special gift- a coat to remind Joseph how much he was loved. How does your family show love to each other?

Some time later, Joseph and the brothers were out in a field. The brothers did an evil thing. They took off Joseph's special robe, then threw Joseph in a deep well! Then they destroyed the robe and told their father that Joseph had been eaten by animals. Finally, they sold Joseph to some slave traders.

We stopped reading in middle of Joseph's story. It seems pretty bad for him right now, but we'll hear the rest in the next chapter. God isn't finished with Joseph. There's more to come!

Look up this memory verse and say it out loud: Acts 7:9-10
"These patriarchs were jealous of their brother Joseph, and they

sold him to be a slave in Egypt. But God was with him and rescued him from all his troubles."

Pray about it: Thank God for our families. Ask God to help you show love to your family today.

Active time!
For many years, people used quilts to save memories. Like Joseph's coat, quilts are colorful ways to wrap someone in love. Fabric was saved from special items- a favorite dress that is now too small, an old blanket, or even favorite bed sheets. Look around- do you have anything that could be used for a family quilt (even old t-shirts work well for this project)? If so, cut squares from the fabric- make sure the squares are the same size. Also, be sure to ask a parent before cutting anything! Then use a sewing machine to sew the fabric squares together like a checkerboard. To complete your quilt, sew one big piece of fabric to the back of your sewn-together squares. No matter how big or small, you've created a blanket of memories!

Alternatives:
-If you don't have used items at home for this project, you can also purchase fabric from a craft store. Another option is to buy old clothes from a thrift store and use pieces of those. Ask family members to each pick one type of fabric. This unique blend will create a blanket that represents your family.
-If you'd like to try a challenge, find quilt patterns and instructions on the internet.
-If sewing is not your thing, you can make a family "quilt" with paper and crayons, markers, colored pencils, or other art supplies.

On each piece of paper, write down and illustrate family memories. When you are finished, tape or staple each piece of paper together in a checkerboard pattern.

Bonus fun: Create puppets out of paper bags, paper cutouts attached to popsicle sticks, socks, or even use dolls or action figures. Tell the story of Joseph as a puppet show.

My Time With God:

Joseph Forgives

The Scripture: Genesis 42:1–45:7

Joseph had quite an exciting life! He grew up in a big family, fighting with a bunch of brothers. He was sold into slavery in a strange country but then served an Egyptian official. Soon, Joseph was rewarded for his hard work. Right when things were going well, he was accused of a crime he didn't do and was thrown into jail!

When he was in jail, he met a cup bearer and baker who had troubling dreams. God helped Joseph tell them what the dream meant. Years later, his good character and God's blessing led him to freedom and leadership. One night, Pharaoh (the guy who ruled over all of Egypt) had a confusing dream and needed to know what it meant. So Joseph was freed from prison so God could help him understand Pharaoh's dream! There was a famine coming to Egypt, and God gave Pharaoh the dream to warn him. A famine is a time when there is no rain, so people can't grow food to eat. God also gave Joseph wisdom to know what to do and showed him how to provide food for all the people. So Pharaoh put Joseph in charge.

In the years to come, Joseph helped saved Egypt from starvation and then was reunited with his family. The brothers traveled to Egypt looking for food. When they met Joseph, he was not angry with them. Instead, he hugged them and cried and told them he forgave them. Then he invited his whole family to come live with him in Egypt. Whew! Did you get all that?

Even though Joseph's brothers did some very mean things to him, Joseph still forgave them. Then he did an incredible thing. Joseph showed he loved his brothers by providing food for them when they needed it most. How do you think it felt for Joseph to do that? Can you imagine how his brothers felt?

It's not easy to forgive each other, especially when we feel hurt or angry. But our love for each other is much, much bigger than hurt feelings. And it's important that other people know how much we love them. How can we show love and forgiveness when we are mad?

When we look at Joseph's story, we see how God used every single part of it for a reason- even the bad parts. But, we have the advantage to see the entire story all at one time. Joseph only knew his past and present. How do you think he felt when he only knew the hard parts? Do you think he would have felt differently if he knew the good things that were coming?

God has big plans and purposes for your life, too. Though you can only see your past and present right now, the big picture is a perfect design by God. Have hope and joy as you trust God for the amazing blessings that are on their way!

Look up this memory verse and say it out loud: Colossians 3:13b "Forgive as the Lord forgave you."

Pray about it: Thank God for His perfect plan! Ask Him to help you see where He is directing your life. Then, thank God for loving and forgiving us. Ask Him to help you show love and forgiveness to others this week.

Active time!
Is there someone you need to forgive? Write a note or draw a picture to show them you forgive them and love them. If you feel really creative, add some cookies, fresh flowers, or another treat. Love and forgiveness are always best!

Bonus fun: Become a Kindness Secret Agent. Do something extra nice for a sibling (or a cousin or a friend if you're an only child). But, if they catch you in the act, you have to do another nice thing in secret once you finish the original nice surprise!

<u>My Time With God:</u>

Baby Moses

The Scripture: Exodus 2:1-10

Hundreds of years passed after the days of Joseph and Egypt had a new Pharaoh. No one remembered Joseph, and they made all of God's people slaves. It was a hard time for the Israelites. Pharaoh made a horrible rule. He said that all baby boys that were born to Israelites had to die.

One woman had a baby boy that she loved very much. She decided to hide him so he could live. She knew she could not keep him hidden forever, so when he was only three months old, the woman made a special basket for him. She put the baby in the basket and placed the basket in the river. The baby's older sister, Miriam, kept watch as the basket floated down the river. Before long, it landed near a place where Pharaoh's daughter was bathing in the river. She saw the basket and was surprised to find a baby inside! Pharaoh's daughter kept the baby as her very own son. She named him Moses.

Moses' mom did a very brave thing. It was a dangerous time to have a baby, but Moses' mother kept her son safe. She had to be very creative and take risks, but it saved Moses' life!

Moses probably didn't know about how his mother saved him by floating him down a river in a basket until he was much older. Often, we don't know about all the gifts and sacrifices our parents do for us, either. Moms and dads are always working "behind the scenes" to make sure we have everything we need. Meanwhile, God is our Heavenly Father who also provides for us.

Many years later, God gave Moses the Ten Commandments. One of God's commands was to "honor your father and mother." Sometimes, it can be difficult to honor our parents. We get frustrated with rules or mad when we don't get to do what we want. But, we need to remember to be obedient to God. We can't forget all the "behind the scenes" ways our mother and father love us.

Look up this memory verse and say it out loud: Exodus 20:12 "Honor your father and your mother, so that you may live long in the land the Lord your God is giving you."

Pray about it: Thank God for your parents. Ask Him to bless them, and help you show them extra love this week.

Active time!
Show thankfulness to Mom or Dad this week. Write a note or tell them how much you love them. Thank them specifically for things you appreciate! Or, maybe you'd like to show them by doing something nice, treating them to something special, or making a small gift.

Bonus fun: Have you ever woven a basket? Check out www.artistshelpingchildren.org/paperweavingartscraftsideaskids.html for instructions on making your own basket and other paper-weaving crafts.

My Time With God:

Moses and the Burning Bush

The Scripture: Exodus 3:1-4:17

God had a big job for Moses. He was going to help free the people from slavery in Egypt. It wasn't an easy job, but God thought of all the details. Then He shared those details with Moses! Remember Abraham? God told Abraham and Sarah to start the journey, but didn't give them the whole story right away. Many times, God only tells His people a few details at a time. But Moses got a lot of information right there by a burning bush.

When Moses grew up, he left Egypt and lived in a place called Midian. His job was watching over sheep. One day, he was out in the wilderness with the sheep when he saw an incredible sight. A bush was on fire! But this was no regular bush with regular fire. This bush was not turning to black smoke and ashes the way wood usually burns. So Moses went to get a closer look.

When he got near the burning bush, Moses suddenly heard a voice call his name! It was the Lord, and he told Moses all about the plan to free the Israelites from slavery. Moses would be their leader, and God told him what to do.

But, that information wasn't enough for Moses. He kept thinking of reasons he wasn't good for the job. Have you ever felt that way? When in your life have you felt like you weren't ready to do something someone asked you to do? What reasons did you give for not being good enough?

"But, Lord" seemed to be Moses' favorite thing to say.

Every time Moses said "But, Lord," the Lord had an answer. And it wasn't just any answer- God showed Moses amazing signs like turning his staff into a snake! That should get someone's attention! Yet, after all of that, Moses still said, "Send someone else."

Even though God gave him so much information, Moses really didn't know what he would've missed if he didn't follow God's instructions. Besides helping set the Israelites free, there were many miracles along the way. God had important reasons for choosing Moses to be a leader. He was just the right person for the job. God also made YOU the right person for a job. What do you think that job is? Will you be courageous to follow God's voice even if you think you're not ready?

Look up this memory verse and say it out loud: Exodus 4:12 [The Lord said,] "Now go; I will help you speak and will teach you what to say."

Pray about it: Thank God for giving you a job to do. Ask Him to show you how to serve Him, and to help you be willing to do whatever He asks.

Active time!
Grab some red, yellow, and orange construction paper. Trace your hand on as many pages as you can, then cut them out. On each

hand, write something that makes you unique. It might be where you live, a special talent, something you've learned, or your age. When you've written something on each hand, arranged them and glue or tape them together to make a "burning bush" to place on your wall.

Bonus fun: When Moses stepped close to the burning bush, God told him to remove his shoes because it was holy ground. Spend the whole day without your shoes. When anyone asks you why, tell them the story of Moses and the burning bush.

My Time With God:

Moses and Pharaoh

The Scripture: Exodus 5; 7:14-11:10

Pharaoh liked having slaves. They worked very hard for him, and he didn't even have to pay them! But God did not like that His people were suffering, so something had to change.

God sent Moses to tell Pharaoh to let His people go. Every time Pharaoh said "no", God would send a terrible warning. These warnings were called "plagues". The first time Pharaoh refused to let the people go, God turned all the water into blood. The Pharaoh changed his mind! He said the slaves would be freed, and so God made the water clean again. But Pharaoh changed his mind yet again and decided the people must stay slaves.

So God sent another plague, this time frogs were running around everywhere! Again, Pharaoh said the people could go and the plague stopped. Once everything was normal again, Pharaoh changed his mind and wouldn't release the people. Over and over again this happened, with plagues of gnats, flies, sick cattle, sores on people's skin, hail falling out of the sky, swarms of locusts, and darkness falling over the land. Nothing made Pharaoh keep his word and let the people go.

The last plague was the most terrible. All of the firstborn sons in Egypt died, including Pharaoh's own son. Finally, Pharaoh said the people could go. God took the Israelites safely out of Egypt.

When God has a plan, people can't stop it. God would free his people no matter what Pharaoh did. When God gives us instructions, we do have a choice to say yes or no. But choosing not to follow God ends up being a bad decision. Every time Pharaoh said "no" to God, there was another consequence, and none of them were fun (despite how cool frogs seem, they are smelly and germy and croak so loud you can't sleep).

Also, Pharaoh wasn't the only one who suffered through the plagues. His bad decisions affected all of his people. When we choose not to follow God's way, our decisions matter to the people around us, too. Has that ever happened to you? Who do your decisions affect? Have you ever had to face consequences for someone else's choice, either good or bad?

Look up this memory verse and say it out loud: Psalm 119:30 "I have chosen the way of faithfulness; I have set my heart on your laws."

Pray about it: Thank God for helping us make good choices. Ask Him to show you how to follow Him today and all week.

Active time!
Head to the library or check out internet resources, and learn about ancient Egypt and Pharaohs! What new, interesting facts can you find? Many historians think Thutmose II was Pharaoh when Moses was alive. Can you find any information on this?

Bonus fun: Be an Egyptian builder. Use clay to make your own miniature pyramids, or even the Sphinx.

My Time With God:

The Red Sea

The Scripture: Exodus 12:31-39; 13:17-14:31

The Israelites were free from Pharaoh, and on their way to the land God promised them. But uh oh! Pharaoh changed his mind again and sent his army after God's people. As the army got closer, the Israelites found themselves at the edge of the Red Sea. It looked like there was no way out. The Israelites were caught between a sea and an army. What would God do?

Of course, God rescued them. And He did it in a way that no one expected. God told Moses to raise his staff, then God parted the waters of the Red Sea and made a way for His people to walk to the other side! He kept all of the Israelites safe as they crossed to safety. Can you imagine what it was like to walk on dry land between two large walls of ocean water?

Sometimes, we find ourselves in situations that seem hopeless. We can't think of a possible way that they will turn out well. However, we are loved by a God who can do anything! Just because we can't imagine a good ending to our problems doesn't mean that God doesn't have a better idea. How do you think the Israelites felt as they stood on the shore of the Red Sea with the Egyptian army racing toward them? Have you ever felt hopeless and scared? What did God do? How did things work out?

The next time a difficult situation happens, be on the lookout for a miracle from God!

Look up this memory verse and say it out loud: Ephesians 3:20-21
"Now to Him who is able to do immeasurably more than all we ask or imagine, according to His power that is at work within us, to Him be glory in the church and in Christ Jesus throughout all generations, for ever and ever! Amen."

Pray about it: Thank God for parting the Red Sea and for miracles that still happen today. Ask Him to show you the way through your next problem.

Active time!
Read about Jewish Passover, a celebration and observation based on the Exodus story. A parent can help you find unleavened bread or matzo crackers at your local grocery store, or use a recipe to make your own. You might even try the other herbs and foods found on the Passover plate as you remember their meanings in the story.

Bonus fun: Create your own board game where the Israelites have to avoid the plagues, cross the sea, and make it safely out of Egypt!

My Time With God:

Israelites in the Wilderness

The Scripture: Exodus 16

The Israelites escaped Egypt, crossed the Red Sea, and traveled through the desert in search of the Promised Land. There wasn't much to eat in the wilderness, so God provided food for them. God gave them manna, a substance they could grind and bake into bread. He also gave them quail, a bird they could eat for meat.

God provided this food daily (though twice as much before the Sabbath so they could rest that day). They were given very specific instructions: "only gather enough for your family for the day." If they gathered more, the food would spoil and rot.

God wanted the people to trust Him. They needed to believe that there would be just enough food every day, and rely on Him to feed their hunger. Though we aren't roaming the desert and given a daily miracle for our food, God still provides for us. He also wants us to trust Him just as much as the Israelites did. We get to trust Him to provide our food, water, clothes, shelter, and anything else we need.

Since God gives us so many things, we can also share with someone who doesn't have as much. When people share, that is another way God provides enough food, clothes, and other things to everyone. What can you share to help God provide for someone this week?

Look up this memory verse and say it out loud: Philippians 4:19 "But my God shall supply all your needs according to God's riches in glory by Christ Jesus."

Pray about it: Thank God for giving us exactly enough. Ask Him to help you share His provision with someone in need.

Active time!
Work together to make a list of all the things God provides for your family. Place your list on the refrigerator so everyone can see it. You can also add items to the list during the week. Each day, say a prayer of thanks for God's provision of just enough. And if you have more than enough, with whom can you share?

Bonus fun: The Israelites wandered in the desert for forty years before they reached the Promised Land. How far do you walk in a day? Ask Mom or Dad if they have a pedometer, FitBit, or other step counter. See how many steps you can take!

<u>My Time With God:</u>

Joshua, Caleb, and the Spies

The Scripture: Number 13:1–3, 17–33; 14:1–11

After wandering the desert, the Israelites were getting very close to the land of Canaan. The Lord told Moses to send men to explore the land. Twelve men went, including Joshua and Caleb.

When they returned from their mission, they told the Israelites about the things they saw. They said the land was very good, full of fruit, and flowing with milk and honey. But the people who lived there were powerful and large. Most of the spies said that it would impossible to take over the land, because the people there were so strong. But Joshua and Caleb had other ideas. They believed that the Israelites would be able to go into the land, because God was with them. Sadly, the people agreed with the other ten spies and they did not want to go into the land of Canaan.

There's a lot happening in this story. We can look at it from three different angles and learn three different things!

1. Look through the eyes of the spies. They went to scout the land God promised. They saw a lot of obstacles and doubted that they would be able to move in and claim the area as their own. These men really thought they were doing the right thing. They wanted

to keep everyone safe and be smart. But, while they worried about that, they stopped trusting God.

2. Look through Joshua and Caleb's eyes. They saw the same things as the other spies, but they saw God's promise, too. They remembered all of the miracles that God already did and trusted that He would make this work, too. But, Joshua and Caleb had to be strong and stand up for truth, even though they were outnumbered by all the other spies.

3. Look through the eyes of the Israelites. They couldn't see the land for themselves. They had to make a decision based on what they heard from Joshua and Caleb, the other spies, and God. They were probably worried about the safety of their families and wanted to make the right choice.

How would you feel if you were each of these people? Do you ever feel this way in your life? Have you ever had to make a decision like the Israelites? Have you stood up for truth when it was unpopular like Joshua and Caleb?

How will this story change your point of view?

Look up this memory verse and say it out loud: Numbers 14:8 "If the Lord is pleased with us, He'll lead us into that land... He'll give it to us."

Pray about it: Thank God for helping us make good choices. Ask God to help you trust Him no matter what happens.

Active time!

Joshua, Caleb, and the spies had to use their observation skills to learn everything they could about the Promised Land. How good are your observation skills? Pick a room in your house or a place like the park, and look around. Notice every detail possible and write them down. Then, like a journalist, write a news story about what you saw.

Bonus fun: What do you think the Promised Land looked like to Joshua, Caleb, and the other spies? Use paper, crayons, markers, or colored pencils to draw a picture of how you think the Promised Land looked.

My Time With God:

Gideon

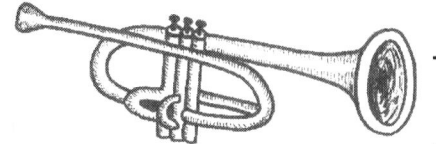

The Scripture: Judges 6-7

Just like Moses, Gideon didn't feel like he was good enough to do the job the Lord gave him. But, unlike Moses, Gideon was ready to go as soon the Lord promised He'd be with him!

The Israelites had trouble with people called the Midianites, who were bullying God's people. The Midianites were a big problem that needed a big solution. They had a large army, so it must take an even larger army to defeat them, right? But really, it would take a very mighty God.

The Lord chose Gideon - a farmer from a small family- specifically to be His leader. Then, He gave Gideon a very small army of men to do the fighting. The reason God did this was important. He wanted to make sure that everyone from Israel to Midian and beyond knew that it wasn't Israel's strength that won the battle. All the credit and glory was for Almighty God.

Gideon followed God's instructions, and each man in the army a trumpet and jar with a torch inside. At the right time, they all smashed their jars and blew the trumpets. The Midianites were so scared and confused, they fought with each other! The Israelites won the day with God's help.

The Lord wants to do big things with us, too. Sometimes, it's the very little things about us that make it easier for other people to see how big God is. When the Lord helps us do things that are more than we could do on our own, He gets glory! Do you have big dreams that you think are impossible to do someday? Those very dreams could be there because God has them planned for you. Don't give up and don't doubt. Instead, ask God how He wants to use you to do big things.

Look up this memory verse and say it out loud: 2 Corinthians 12:9-10
"But He said to me, "My grace is sufficient for you, for my power is made perfect in weakness." Therefore I will boast all the more gladly about my weaknesses, so that Christ's power may rest on me. That is why, for Christ's sake, I delight in weaknesses, in insults, in hardships, in persecutions, in difficulties. For when I am weak, then I am strong."

Pray about it: Thank God for doing big things in little you. Ask God to help you see His vision for you, and know what to do to serve Him well.

Active time!
Make your own lantern torch! Check out this easy to make lantern at www.wikihow.com/Make-a-Kids-Craft-Lantern or search for another idea in a book or online. You can even put a battery-operated candle inside to help light a dark room. You can also roll up a piece of paper to use as a "trumpet" with your Gideon lantern!

Bonus fun: Before God rescued them, the Israelites spent a lot of time hiding from the Midianites. Now is a great time to play "hide and seek" with family members or friends. But first, tell them about the day Gideon stopped hiding and started following the Lord.

My Time With God:

Samson

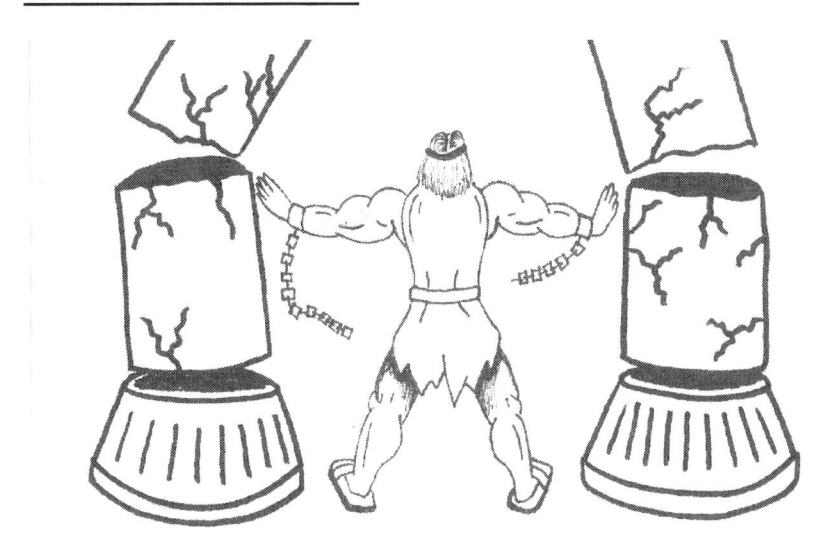

The Scripture: Judges 13:2-7,24; 16:4-30

When Samson was a baby, God gave him a special gift of strength. God had big plans for Samson to grow up and lead the Israelites.

God gives everyone special talents and gifts. What do you think He gave you and the people in your family? God wants us all to use these gifts to bless Him and give Him glory.

However, Samson didn't always make good decisions and sometimes used his strength in ways that didn't please God.

As a reminder that God was the source of Samson's strength, God told Samson not to cut his hair. Samson didn't keep that promise, either. He let himself be tricked by his a woman named Delilah so she could turn him over to his enemies. Since Samson didn't honor his promise to God and he let his hair be cut, God removed

Samson's strength. Samson couldn't fight off his enemies and was taken prisoner.

Samson's story didn't end with bad decisions. Though he had to deal with the consequences of his actions, God forgave Samson and restored his strength. The last thing Samson did was use his God-given strength to overpower Israel's enemies. Samson was still able to be used by God one last time. It's never too late to do good things for God.

Look up this memory verse and say it out loud: Judges 16:28 "[Samson] said, "Lord and King, show me that you still have concern for me. God, please make me strong just one more time."

Pray about it: Thank God for giving us strength, gifts, and talents. Ask the Lord to help you use your strengths, gifts, and talents to please Him.

Active time!
How strong are you? Exercise and build your strength today! Run, do sit ups, push-ups, and jumping jacks. Then stretch or even lift weights. Exercising every day builds strength, and who knows, maybe you'll be strong like Samson one day!

Bonus fun: Do you know what talents and gifts God gave you? Write them down! Sometimes it's easier for other people to see your gifts, so ask a friend or family member if you need ideas. Next, can you think of ways you are using these gifts for God? This can be things you do at church or things you do to share Christ at school or with friends. Finally, what is one thing you can do this week to use your talents to please God?

My Time With God:

Ruth

The Scripture: Ruth 1:1-2:23; 4:13-17

Think about each person in your family, and how much you love them. If any of them moved away, would you want to go with them?

Of course! We love and care about the people in our family, and we want to be near them. Ruth felt the same way about her mother-in-law, Naomi. Naomi was moving from where they lived in Moab to her original home in Bethlehem. Ruth wanted to move to Bethlehem with her mother-in-law. She knew that moving away with Naomi would mean not having very much to eat or a husband to take care of her, but her love for Naomi was much more important.

When they were in Bethlehem, Ruth and Naomi needed to find something to eat. Ruth went out to a field to collect scraps that the harvesters dropped and left behind. While she was there, she met the man who owned the field. His name was Boaz, and he was very kind to Ruth.

When Ruth first met Boaz, she didn't know that he was Naomi's cousin. What a surprise! Boaz and Ruth fell in love. Boaz showed love for family by marrying Ruth and taking care of her (and Naomi, too!). There are many ways to show our family members that we love them, from giving hugs to taking care of needs like food and clothing. How do you show love to your family? How do they show love to you?

Look up this memory verse and say it out loud: Ephesians 4:2 "Be completely humble and gentle; be patient, bearing with one another in love."

Pray about it: Thank God for the ways He shows us love. Ask God to help you share His love in active ways to your family today.

Active time!
This week, connect with a family member who lives far away or you haven't seen lately. Send a card or a letter, or some updated pictures of your family. You can also send a care package of cookies, drawings, or crafts you made. Tell grandparents, aunts, uncles, or cousins about the story of Ruth and how God loves families.

Bonus fun: Ruth gathered grain from the field, which could be made into bread. You don't have to grind your own grain, but ask an adult for help in finding a simple bread recipe and making a loaf of your very own.

<u>My Time With God:</u>

Samuel Hears God

SAMUEL!   **The Scripture**: 1 Samuel 3:1-10

Samuel was just a kid when he moved to the temple. He spent his days learning about God and serving Him. But this was the first time Samuel heard the Lord's voice. At first, Samuel didn't recognize who was speaking because he had never heard God before. What do you think His voice sounded like to Samuel?

Samuel thought the priest, Eli, was calling him. So he went to ask Eli what he needed. After this happened a couple of times, Eli realized that God was calling Samuel. He told Samuel to say, "Speak, Lord, for your servant is listening." That's just what Samuel did, and so God spoke to Samuel and told him what to do to serve Him.

Guess what? God still speaks to us today! While He can certainly speak out loud, He also chooses to speak to us through other ways. We can hear God through signs, dreams, another person, or directly through His words in the Bible. But unless we are familiar with His voice, we won't recognize it when we hear it. The way to get to know God is to spend time with Him! The more time we spend reading His Word, praying, and worshiping, the more familiar we will be with the Lord's voice.

Meanwhile, when we look around church, home, and school, we see grown-ups doing many things. Adults teach, preach, lead music, take offering, pray, and more. But what things do you see kids doing?

Samuel started serving God when he was very young. There were things he could do in the temple even though he was a child. In fact, God spoke to Samuel even though Samuel was still a kid!

Any kid today can be like Samuel, even you! What kind of things do you think you can do to help serve the Lord, both in and out of church? God also speaks to children, just like He speaks to adults. We just need to practice listening.

Look at this week's verse. It says, "AS Samuel grew up," not "WHEN Samuel grew up." God doesn't want us to wait until we're adults to hear God's voice. He wants us to listen today.

Look up this memory verse and say it out loud: 1 Samuel 3:19a "As Samuel grew up, the Lord was with him."

Pray about it: Thank God for speaking to us in many ways. Ask God to show you how to serve Him no matter how old you are.

Active time!
Grab a puzzle and start putting it together. While you're working, think about how Samuel had to figure out the puzzle of Who was speaking to him at night. He put together the information he knew of God, what Eli told him, and what the Lord was saying. You can make your own puzzle out of cardboard or paper, and perhaps draw of a picture from our story.

Bonus fun: Find a buddy to play some listening games!

1. One person wears a blindfold while the other person makes sounds (opening a door, crunching food, rubbing cloth together... be creative!). The blindfolded person guesses the sounds.

2. Try to make a homemade phone using string between two cups or cans.

3. Play "telephone" with friends or family: whisper secrets to each other, and see if the message stays clear after being passed around to each person.

<u>My Time With God:</u>

Samuel Appoints David

The Scripture: 1 Samuel 16:1-13

Samuel had a big, important job: he had to select the next king. Thankfully, God did the hard part. God already knew who would be the best person to lead the people. Samuel only needed to listen and obey His instructions.

When you think of a king, what do you imagine? Describe what you think a king is like.

The people in this story, including Samuel, also had an idea of who they thought the next king would be. So Samuel followed God's direction and traveled to Bethlehem to choose the new king. When he got there, God led him to a man named Jesse who had many sons. Samuel thought that the oldest son would make a good king, but God said, "The Lord doesn't look at thing things that people see. People look at the outside, but the Lord looks at a person's heart."

So Samuel saw all of Jesse's many sons, but none of them was the right person to be king. Finally, he met the youngest son, David, who had been out taking care of the family's sheep. God surprised them by choosing David, who was younger and different than the people's idea of a leader. But, the Lord could see who David was on the inside. He knew that David had a good heart and would one day be a great king for the people.

Have you ever been surprised that a person was not who you thought they would be? Were you disappointed or was it a good surprise? What did you see on the outside, and what do you think God saw on the inside of this person?

Look up this memory verse and say it out loud: 1 Samuel 16:7 "People look at the outward appearance, but the Lord looks at the heart."

Pray about it: Thank God for seeing our hearts. Ask God to help you see other people the way He sees them.

Active time!
Create a self-portrait! Using your favorite art supplies, draw a picture of yourself. However, draw the way you think God sees you, and not what you see on the outside!

Bonus fun: Here's a fun game to share with friends or family: Fill a plate or tray with objects (or place a group of objects on the table), anything from around the house. Cover the whole plate or tray with a cloth. Everyone gets 45 seconds to look at the objects before they are covered again. Ask them to name as many objects as they remember. Do this again with different objects, but this time, only feel them from under the cover. Then try to name as many as possible. Which was easier and which was harder? How was it different to see or feel? How can this help us remember our story about God being able to see the inside of a person?

My Time With God:

David the Shepherd

The Scripture: Psalm 23

Before it was time for David to become a king, he was still a shepherd boy. A shepherd had the important job of minding the family's sheep. However, it wasn't usually a very exciting job.

Shepherds kept all the sheep together and safe. Sometimes this meant fighting or scaring away predators that could harm the flock. Shepherds also made sure to lead the flock of sheep to places where there was plenty of grass to eat and water to drink from a pond or stream.

But sheep don't usually move very quickly, so shepherds also had time just to sit and watch. This gave David time to think, and he thought about how God was like a shepherd. Years later, David wrote a song about this. He reminded us how God takes care of our needs, keeps us safe, and even disciplines us like a shepherd teaches sheep how to obey. What other ways is the Lord like a shepherd? (Make sure you read Psalm 23 for ideas!)

Look up this memory verse and say it out loud: Psalm 23:1-3
"The Lord is my shepherd, I lack nothing. He makes me lie down in green pastures, he leads me beside quiet waters, he refreshes my soul. He guides me along the right paths for His name's sake."

Pray about it: Thank God for being a good Shepherd. Ask God to help you see the many ways He cares for you.

Active time!

Visit the library or get a parent's permission to research on the internet. Learn everything you can about sheep and how to take care of them. How does this help you understand David's job and the way he says God is like a good shepherd?

Bonus fun: Make your own flock of sheep using cotton balls, pipe cleaners, or any other craft supplies you have. Add googly eyes to make silly sheep. You might also use craft sticks to build a sheep pen for your cotton flock!

My Time With God:

David and Goliath

The Scripture: 1 Samuel 17:1-50

Have you ever been bullied? Has someone ever been mean to you or made fun of you? What was that like?

The Israelites were at war with people called the Philistines. The Philistine army had a certain soldier named Goliath. Goliath was a pretty intimidating guy. He was huge! People called him a giant! And Goliath was mean. He yelled, insulted, and taunted the Israelites to send someone to fight.

Sometimes, it feels like people at school or on the playground are like Goliath. Their words can be very cruel and they never seem to stop. So what do we do?

David's brothers were part of the Israelite army. One day, David went to visit them and he heard Goliath yelling. When he found out about Goliath's meanness, he said, "Who defies the army of the living God?" David, with God's help, would fight Goliath.

When David met Goliath, he followed God's instructions. In his case, it was to kill him with a slingshot because they were at war. Of course, we don't want to hurt the bullies in our lives! But we can still learn from David. Goliath didn't pick on only David, he was yelling at the Israelite army. Like David, we can stand up to bullies even if they are mean to someone else. We can do the right thing to help other people who are being bullied.

The most important thing that David did was to do things God's way. Originally, King Saul wanted him to wear his army, but it didn't fit! Instead of wearing King Saul's armor and carrying a heavy sword, David remembered all the things he learned while growing up. We need to remember all the things we learn about sharing God's love. When we love bullies like God loves us, everybody wins. How can YOU share God's love with someone who is being a bully? What will you do next time that happens?

David wasn't a powerful person on his own, and especially not up against a giant warrior like Goliath. But, David knew the best power source ever- God!

We know that a lamp doesn't work unless it's plugged into a wall and our phone or video games need a battery. Just like those things that need a power source, we need God's power to win battles big and small. Are you full of God's power? If so, how do you know? And if not, can you ask God to fill you with strength? Ask Him to fill you with so much of His love that you can share Him with any bullies you meet, too.

Look up this memory verse and say it out loud: Romans 12:21 "Don't let evil defeat you, but defeat evil with good."

Pray about it: Thank God for the power of the Holy Spirit and His great love. Ask God to fill you with strength and love this week and show you how to share it with others.

Active time!
Develop a bully action plan! Work together with a parent or teacher to decide how to share God's love when being bullied or

standing up for someone who is bullied. Talk about staying safe, avoiding fights, and how to win with God's goodness.

Bonus fun: Create a giant Goliath out of paper and put him on the wall. Using rolled up socks as "stones" see if you can hit Goliath on the head from various places in the room.

<u>My Time With God:</u>

Rebuilding the Temple

The Scripture: Nehemiah 1-4; 7:1-4; 8:1-5

Nehemiah lived in a sad time for the people of God. There had been many battles, and the Israelites were taken away and placed in other countries. But God was faithful to His promises and, after many years, it was time to go back home.

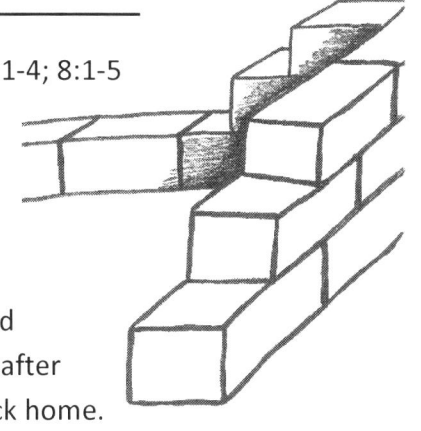

Of course, a lot had changed in the decades since the Israelites left Jerusalem. The temple and the walls of the city had to be rebuilt. It wasn't an easy job because they still had enemies who tried to stop them. The enemies would make fun of them, threatened to attack them, and made it harder to build the wall. But the Israelites cried out to God and worked with all their heart.

But we know that nothing is too hard for God! The people worked together and followed God's commands until the work was finished. The wall was rebuilt! We can learn many things from their story.

What can did you learn about teamwork and trusting God?

What can you learn about encouraging someone who has a difficult challenge?

When we work together with all the unique talents God gave us, we make a good team!

Look up this memory verse and say it out loud: Nehemiah 8:10b: "The joy of the Lord is your strength."

Pray about it: Thank God for helping us face difficult challenges together. Ask God to help you be a good teammate to others.

Active time!
Build a wall while you think about what happened in Jerusalem. Use pillows, blankets, couch cushions, empty boxes, or anything else you have that is soft and safe. You might even turn your wall into a fort!

Bonus fun: Find a friend, sibling, or other family members and build something as a team. You can create a tent or treehouse, do a puzzle, build a model, or even make a meal. Be creative and work together!

<u>My Time With God:</u>

Esther

The Scripture: Esther 2:2-18; 4:1-5:8; 7:1-6

Can you imagine what it would be like to be Esther? One day, the king called for all the young, beautiful women in the kingdom to come to the palace. He was looking for a new queen. So, Esther had to leave her home and go to the palace where she didn't know anyone and life was very different. Have you ever been anywhere different or unfamiliar? What did that feel like?

Then, Esther was chosen to be queen! This was exciting and probably a little bit overwhelming, too. But soon, things got scary. Queen Esther found out that someone in the palace, named Haman, had bad plans for God's people. It would be very risky to try to stop these plans. But God helped Queen Esther, and He saved the day! Queen Esther had dinner with the King and Haman. There, she bravely told the king that she was one of God's people and that Haman needed to be stopped. The king listened and changed the laws so that God's people and Queen Esther would be safe.

At first, Esther didn't know why her life changed so much. In fact, she might have wished to stay home and never go to the palace at all. But God had plans for Esther and all of His people. He needed someone close to the king in order to keep the people safe. Esther was in the right place at the right time. She was in God's place in God's time!

Look up this memory verse and say it out loud: Esther 4:14 "Who knows? It's possible that you became queen for a time just like this."

Pray about it: Thank God for His perfect plan. Ask God what He wants you to do in this very time and place.

Active time!
Did you know that God put you in the right place at the right time? And He has a job for you. Think about where you live, who you see, and what things are special about you. Is there some way to serve God that you can do better than anyone else? Can you reach out to someone that no one else can? Talk with a friend or family member, pray together, and be on the lookout for God's purpose for you!

Bonus fun: Esther lived in a pretty simple home until she was chosen to come to the king's fancy palace. What a big change! If you have blocks or lego bricks, build the biggest castle you can as you think about Queen Esther's story.

My Time With God:

Job

The Scripture: Job 1-2; 42:7-17

We've all had some pretty bad days, but Job might've had the worst of them all. His life was pretty good, and certainly happy. Then, suddenly, everything changed. Job lost his family and his farm. He got sores all over his body. Job was in pain, heartbroken, sad, and confused. He didn't understand why he suddenly lost everything important to him.

However, the most important thing to Job was the Lord. Job still had God, even when his other friends left him. God stayed by Job's side through all the sad days and hard times. He never left Job for a single minute!

Job had so many questions about his problems. God listened to every single question for as long as Job needed to talk. Then, God answered Job. He also restored all of the things Job lost when the time was right. Job probably still had sadness about the things and people he missed, but he knew God was still in charge and everything would be alright.

Have you ever had a day when everything went wrong? How did you handle it? What would you say to God about it?

To find out what happened to Job, read today's scriptures in your Bible!

Look up this memory verse and say it out loud: Job 19:25
"I know that my redeemer lives, and that in the end he will stand on the earth."

Pray about it: Thank God for being there on bad days. Ask God to help you see His plan when life is hard.

Active time!
Question time! Do you have questions for God? Write them down. See how many questions or pages of questions you can think of to ask the Lord. They can be serious or silly, happy or sad, curious or even angry. If you feel brave, you can share your list with a parent, teacher, or pastor. They might have some answers and pray with you about your big questions.

Bonus fun: Job's friends tried to help him, but they weren't very comforting. Can you think of ways they could've been better friends? How can you be a good friend to someone who is hurting? Think of someone you know who is sad, sick, or injured. Now, think of ways you can comfort or cheer them. Be a good friend to someone in need.

My Time With God:

Psalm 19

The Scripture: Psalm 19

The book of Psalms is made up of songs that David and others wrote. David was a musician, so these songs had a melody. Since we don't know how they sounded, they are like poetry for us. How do you think this psalm sounded? Can you try singing the words?

Let's look closely at Psalm 19. The first part talks about God's creation of nature. David says even the sky and the heavens declare God's glory. How do you think this happens since things in nature can't talk? What things remind you of God?

The next section says that God's law is perfect and continues to describe good things about God's commands. What do you think of this? We don't always like rules made by people, but do you like rules made by God? What makes God's laws good?

God's laws are instructions for a blessed life. When we follow God's commands, we can be happy and make good decisions. We will grow closer to God and we will become more mature and loving. No wonder David loved God's laws so much!

Look up this memory verse and say it out loud: Psalm 19:7 "The law of the Lord is perfect, refreshing the soul."

Pray about it: Thank God for His law. Ask God to help you remember and follow His commands.

Active time!
Let's practice following and loving God's law. Think about three of God's commands. You can look in your Bible for some ideas or use some of the Ten Commandments. Then write the three you've chosen on a piece of paper and post it somewhere you and your family will see it all week. Help each other follow God's instructions, lovingly reminding and encouraging each other!

Bonus fun: The beginning of Psalm 19 says that the heavens declare the glory of the Lord. Use your research skills and learn more about God's creation in space. Read about stars, planets, comets, and more. How do you think the heavens declare the glory of the Lord?

My Time With God:

Psalm 34

The Scripture: Psalm 34

David's life had many challenges. Often, he was running away from enemies who wanted to kill him! But God remained faithful to David and kept him safe from harm. Sometimes, this involved a little bit of creativity. Once, David acted like he was crazy, which made his enemy run away! He wrote this psalm after that happened.

Even though David had been in a very stressful situation, he still worshiped God. The first lines of this song (remember, the psalms are songs) are all about praising the Lord. The word "extol" means to praise or exalt. Some translations of the Bible use the word "magnify" instead of "glorify". Both words are similar in meaning, but can you imagine trying to magnify the Lord? How could we make Him any bigger than He already is?

In this psalm, David wants everyone to know how great God is. That's what he means by glorify or magnify the Lord- making God's name known to all people. This could mean praising God so much that it makes people pay attention! Have you ever praised God so enthusiastically that everyone noticed? How could this kind of worship bring glory to God?

Look up this memory verse and say it out loud: Psalm 34:3
"Glorify the Lord with me; let us exalt His name together."

Pray about it: Thank God for His goodness in stressful times. Ask God to help you magnify His name so much that other people praise Him, too.

Active time!
Find a magnifying glass and do some exploring around your house or neighborhood. How different do things look when they are bigger? Do you notice anything you've missed before? How is magnifying the Lord similar to magnifying the objects around you?

Bonus fun: Using a book or the internet with a parent's permission, find super magnified pictures. It's a challenge to identify objects when you only get a close-up view. This is because we can see details we've never been able to look at with just our eyes. What new details about God can we discover when we glorify Him?

My Time With God:

Psalm 47

The Scripture: Psalm 47

Praising God can be fun! The book of Psalms is full of exciting ways to praise the Lord. People praise Him by singing, dancing, playing instruments, and shouting. What is your favorite way to worship God?

What do you think "praising God" means? When we praise someone, we tell them the good things about something they've done or who they are. There are plenty of good things to say about who God is or what He does. How many reasons can you think of to praise our Lord?

Though it's possible to praise quietly, God is so big and amazing that He is worthy of much rejoicing! Just like the people who wrote the psalms, we can make God happy by praising with a joyful noise.

Look up this memory verse and say it out loud: Psalm 13:6
"I will sing the Lord's praise, for He has been good to me."

Pray about it: Tell God everything you think is good about Him. Ask God to help you praise Him joyfully this week.

Active time!
Praise God in a new way this week! Learn a new praise song to sing in the car, make simple instruments (like small objects in a bottle to shake, a drum out of an overturned plastic container, or any other creative idea), write a poem about God's goodness, or

even make up a dance to your favorite praise song. Can you think of any other ways to praise God? You can try them all!

Bonus fun: Have you ever been to a sporting event or game where there were cheerleaders? Their enthusiasm gets the whole crowd to cheer together! Make up a cheer for God. It can rhyme or not, be simple or complex, or have clapping and dance moves if you want. Whatever you do, be energetic and joyful as you bring praise to our Mighty God.

My Time With God:

Psalm 139

The Scripture: Psalm 139

The Bible is full of amazing stories of God and His people. What's your favorite Bible story?

Those stories happened a long time ago, and can feel very different from our lives today. But, God's story doesn't end when we turn the last page of the Bible. The story continues today! And you are a very special part of it.

Psalm 139 says that God knew about every minute of your life before you were even born. Everything about you is important to Him- when you're asleep or awake, lying down or sitting up- everything! He loves you so much!

Just like Moses, David, Queen Esther, Paul, and all the rest, God has a place for you in His plan. None of our Bible heroes were superhuman. They were all just ordinary people like me and you. But, we become extraordinary when we're filled with the Holy Spirit and follow God's plan. And just like God was with all of our Bible heroes, He is with you.

We often say that God is everywhere. But have you ever thought about what that really means? In this scripture, the psalmist thinks about the farthest places of earth and heaven. It's easy to picture God in His big creation, places we can't even visit. What does "everywhere" look like for your family? Is it the home of a distant relative or a far-away country? What about closer locations, like at school, work, or home? Yes, God is even in the bathroom (go ahead and laugh)!

Most importantly, God is always with us, no matter what happens. God really is everywhere. God is with us when we get a good surprise and we are happy. God is with us when something terrible happens and we are sad. He is with us when we are scared, and He's with us to show us the way when things are new and different. What other times or places is God with us? Where do you think you fit into God's story? What do you imagine God might have planned for your life?

Look up this memory verse and say it out loud: Psalm 139:16 "You saw me before I was born. Every day of my life was written in your book... before a single day had passed."

Pray about it: Thank God for His great story. Ask Him to help you see your place in His story. Also, thank the Lord for being everywhere and ask Him to help you see Him all the time.

Active time!
Make a story book! Write your story with God. Include your heritage, when you learned about Christ, and the blessings God has given you. Leave space to add more of your story as it unfolds. You can write your story on the computer and print it out, or make a homemade book with construction paper and staples. Will you draw pictures or write a novel? Your story book is as unique as you, but it will be something special to keep and reread each year.

Bonus fun: The verses in the book of Psalms are poetry and song lyrics. Based on this week's verses and what we've learned about psalms, write a Psalm for you and your family that reflects God's presence. Be creative! It can rhyme, or it can be free-flowing. You might make a song out of it like the original psalms. Choose words that help you see where God is in your life. When you're done, place your Psalm where it can be seen it through the week and be reminded that God is everywhere.

My Time With God:

Proverbs- Friends

The Scripture: Proverbs 17:17, 27:17, Ecclesiastes 4:9-10, and John 15:12-15

The book of Proverbs is full of wise sayings and many of them are written by King Solomon. Solomon was King David's son, and he followed God's way for most of his life. One day, God offered to give Solomon anything he wanted and Solomon chose to ask for God's wisdom. This made God very happy, and Solomon used this wisdom to be a good king.

Proverbs 17:17 talks about some of our favorite people- our friends. This verse reminds us that friends stick together through good times and bad times. No matter what, friends love each other. When we have bad days, that's often the time we need the love of our friends the most.

Proverbs 27:17 uses symbolism to help us understand how friends help each other. When someone wants to sharpen a knife, they can rub another knife or piece of metal along the edge. Just like two pieces of metal can sharpen each other, two friends can help each other learn and grow. What have you learned from your friends? How have you helped your friends follow God's way?

Our verses in Ecclesiastes are about teamwork. It says that two people are better than one, because they can work together. Meanwhile, the scripture in John reminds us of our very best friend- Jesus. Jesus loved us so very much that He died on the cross to forgive our sins and mistakes. He gave everything He had so that we can be close to God. Think about what you know about the way Jesus loves and cares for us. What do we have in common with His way of friendship and how we love and care for our friends?

Look up this memory verse and say it out loud: Proverbs 17:17 "A friend loves at all times, and a brother is born for a time of adversity."

Pray about it: Thank God for being your best and closest friend. Ask Him to help you love your friends the way He loves you.

Active time!
Use cord, embroidery floss, beads, or other craft supplies to make friendship bracelets or keychains for you and your friends. How many friends can you bless this way? Make sure to tell them how Jesus is also their friend when you give them this gift.

Bonus fun: Share today's scripture with a friend. Together, find creative ways to memorize at least one verse. Can you do something fun, like write a song or rap to help you remember? Can you make a sign to display your memory verse somewhere? What about hand or body motions to go with each word? Together, do whatever it takes to remember what the Bible says about friendship!

<u>My Time With God:</u>

Proverbs- Ants

The Scripture: Proverbs 6:6-8, Proverbs 30:25

Did you know the Bible talks about insects? What can we possibly learn from a tiny bug?

You've probably seen an ant before, and you've likely seen many ants all at once! What do you know about these little guys?

While we don't usually like ants in our house or trying to steal our picnic food, they do have a special place in God's world. Ants are pretty strong for their size and can carry objects many times their own weight. They also live and work together in colonies to make sure every ant has enough to eat. Of course, this means every ant has to help do the work.

When we read these verses, we can remember that the entire book of Proverbs teaches wisdom. The ant works hard even though nobody is forcing it. It is wise for us to work hard, too. Ants plan ahead and store food during the summer so they have plenty to eat in the winter. Proverbs says it is wise for us to plan ahead, too.

What do you think we can learn from the ant? What can you do to be more like this hard-working insect?

Look up this memory verse and say it out loud: Colossians 3:23 "Whatever you do, work at it with all your heart, as working for the Lord."

Pray about it: Thank God for teaching us to be wise. Ask God to help you be like an ant this week.

Active time!

Spend some time with ants! Read a book or do some internet research, then check out the ants that live in your own backyard. What do they look like? What do ants like to eat? Are there different kinds of ants around the world? What can we learn from them? After reading our scripture in Proverbs, will you look at ants the same way again?

Bonus fun: Make a special ant snack. The classic "ants on a log" tastes yummy and is healthy, too. Have a grown up help you cut up pieces of celery, then spread peanut butter along one side of each piece. Then, grab some raisins and line them up in the peanut butter like ants marching along a log. If you're allergic to peanut butter, try spreading hummus on the celery instead. Enjoy your delicious ant treat!

My Time With God:

Jonah and the Big Fish

The Scripture: Jonah 1:1-2:1; 2:10-3:10

Jonah was a prophet, which is a person who gives messages from God to His people. God had a message for a town called Nineveh. He wanted Jonah to tell the people to start following God, or their city would be destroyed.

Jonah did not want to give this message, so he tried to run away. Actually, he tried to sail away! But God sent a storm and Jonah was thrown overboard. In the water, he was swallowed by a big fish! He stayed in the fish's stomach for three days and nights, praying to God. Then, the fish spit him up on the shore- right near Nineveh! Jonah obeyed God and told the people what the Lord said. The people did the right thing and praised God!

Jonah's story teaches us many things. First, it shows us what happens when we try to run from God. God is everywhere, and His love won't let us get very far away! Jonah needed a three day time-out in order to think and pray. God will never give up on us, even when we are disobedient to Him. Instead, He helps us grow and follow Him.

Jonah also shows us that our mistakes aren't the end. God always forgives, and He still uses us to complete the jobs He gave us. Even though Jonah got himself in a pretty big mess, God sent His message with Jonah to Nineveh. This helped save the entire city from being destroyed.

Meanwhile, Jonah was in the belly of the big fish for three days before the fish spit him out on the shore. Can you think of someone else who was in a tomb for three days before living again? It's no coincidence that the story of Jonah is similar to Jesus' resurrection. In fact, the New Testament mentions "the sign of Jonah." God wanted everyone to know Jesus was truly the Messiah that the prophecies said would come to save His people. When they saw Jesus was in the tomb three days like Jonah was in the fish, they could know it was a sign from God and believe in His Son.

Look up this memory verse and say it out loud: Jonah 2:9
"I will say, 'Salvation comes from the Lord.'"

Pray about it: Thank God for His patient teaching. Ask God to help you learn more truths from Jonah's story.

Active time!
Many stories about Jonah say he was swallowed by a whale, but the Bible says "big fish". Research the difference between whales and fish. Another theory is that Jonah spent his days in the belly of a large whale shark. What can you find out about them? What do you think about the animal that swallowed Jonah?

Bonus fun: Jonah did NOT want to give God's message to people of Nineveh. He knew the people did not behave in a way that honored God, so he thought the people wouldn't want to hear from the Lord. Does anyone you know remind you of the people of Nineveh? Say a prayer for guidance, then write a letter to that person telling them about the love of Jesus.

My Time With God:

John the Baptist

The Scripture: Matthew 3:1-17

John was Jesus' cousin, and was born only a few months before Him. The Bible tells us about his birth to Zechariah and Elizabeth, even though they were much older than the average parent. When John grew up, he preached in the wilderness and told people about the coming Messiah- his very own cousin, Jesus! Now we see how John baptized Jesus in the Jordan River. After Jesus came up out of the water, the Holy Spirit came down like a dove. God spoke and said, "This is my Son, whom I love; with him I am well pleased."

God chose John the Baptist to prepare people to follow Jesus. John was born especially to accomplish this special task. God gave John all the talents and skills he needed to do this. What kind of skills do you think John the Baptist used to prepare people to follow Jesus?

John isn't the only person God chooses to do special things. Can you think of anyone else in the Bible who did something special for Him?

Do you know what a "purpose" is? A purpose is a reason something exists, or a goal. Did you know that God has a purpose for every person- including you? How exciting to do something special for Him!

Look up this memory verse and say it out loud: Ephesians 2:10 "For we are God's handiwork, created in Christ Jesus to do good works, which God prepared in advance for us to do."

Pray about it: Thank God for giving us the honor of doing special things for Him. Ask God to show you your purpose.

Active time!

Sometimes people know God's purpose for their life and sometimes they are still waiting to discover it. Think about the talents and skills God has given you. What do you dream about for your future? Do you love to sing and dream of being a singer? Perhaps God is calling you to lead worship or make music that praises Him. Do you like to build things and dream of designing houses or cities? Maybe God is preparing you to make homes for people in need! There are no limits to what God can do and how He can use you for a special purpose. Share your dreams and ideas with a friend or family member, and encourage one another to seek God's purpose for your life- starting today!

Bonus fun: You don't need to wait until you're a grown-up to live your purpose. Do one thing right now that gives God glory or serves Him. You can start small and do something kind and loving for someone. Maybe this is a good time to pray for a person in need. Or, can you take something you like to do and use it to praise God or share His love with someone? Put down this book and go give glory to the Lord!

My Time With God:

Jesus is Born

The Scripture: Luke 2:1-20

An angel came to visit a girl named Mary. He told her that she would have a baby and that baby would be God's Son who was coming to save the world. How exciting!

Soon, Mary and her husband Joseph would travel to Bethlehem. The government was counting all the people, so the city was very crowded. There was no place to stay! They found a barn to spend the night, and right there with all the hay and animals, baby Jesus was born!

At the same time, out in the country, there were shepherds. They were watching their sheep, just like they did every night. The only thing different was a really bright star in the sky. Until, suddenly, angels appeared! And they had big news! The Savior everyone was waiting for was born right there in their town!

Of course, the shepherds were so excited that they had to go see the baby at once. They were so happy after they visited Jesus that they couldn't contain themselves. They had to tell everyone the good news about God's Son!

Are you as excited about Jesus as the shepherds were that day? Why or why not? Are you excited enough to share God's good news with everyone you see?

God's love was in Bethlehem that night, and so was the joy of the Lord. The shepherds definitely felt joy when they found out about Jesus. Yes, they were a little scared at seeing a sky full of angels, but the joy happened soon after. And for good reason! God arrived in their little town and they got the first invitation to go see baby Jesus. What do you think it would have been like to be a shepherd that day?

The story of Jesus' birth is incredible. What part is most amazing to you? Do any parts seem difficult to imagine?

God sent Jesus to us on earth because He loves us SO MUCH. God's love is so big, He gave the best gift ever. That gift includes freedom from sin, eternal life in heaven, and God's presence always with us. Someday, we will reach "the end" of this story- happily ever after, living forever surrounded by God's amazing love.

Look up this memory verse and say it out loud: John 3:16
"For God so loved the world that He gave His only begotten Son that whoever believes in Him will not die but have everlasting life."

Pray about it: Thank God for His amazing love and joy! Ask God to help you share that love and joy with the enthusiasm of a Bethlehem shepherd.

Active time!
Nativity scenes are very popular at Christmas. We don't need to wait until December to remember the birth of Jesus. Create your own nativity scene to display today. Start with an empty box. You can stand the box on its side to and decorate it as a stable. Now, create Mary, Joseph, Baby Jesus, shepherds, angels, and animals. Will you draw and cut them out of cardboard and stand them up with craft sticks? Maybe sculpt them out of clay? Glue together different recycled material? Make your nativity scene unique.

Bonus fun: Create a play or musical based on the story of Jesus' birth. Gather your friends or family to play the parts, act it out with dolls or stuffed animals, or write a script like an old-fashioned radio play where you read with different voices and make sound effects.

<u>My Time With God:</u>

Boy Jesus in the Temple

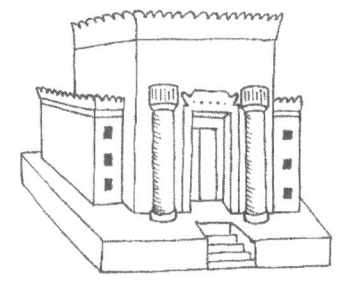

The Scripture: Luke 2:41-52

The story of twelve-year-old Jesus in the temple is the only story we have about Him when He was a kid. It happened when Jesus and his family went to Jerusalem to celebrate Passover. When the festival was over, they began the journey home. But after a day of traveling, Jesus' parents realized that He wasn't with them. They hurried back to Jerusalem and spent days looking for him until they discovered him at the temple spending time with the teachers. When they told Jesus they had been searching for Him, He said, "Didn't you know I had to be in my Father's house?"

What can we learn from this story? We see how Jesus acted as a kid. He was obedient to His parents, even during this mix-up. We don't know how He was separated from Mary and Joseph, but we know from other scriptures that Jesus never did anything wrong. So we can assume that He did not disobey in order to stay in the temple.

Jesus' family was probably traveling in a large group to and from Jerusalem. This is why it took so long for them to notice that Jesus wasn't with them, and why it took so long to find Him in the temple. For three days, Jesus had been hanging out with the teachers! It's important to notice that Jesus was listening to them and asking questions. Even though He amazed everyone with how much He understood, Jesus was humble and respectful, taking the time to hear what the adults explained.

As Christians, our job is to be like Jesus. He gives us a good example of how a kid can be like Him by listening. We can listen to our parents and be obedient. We can also listen when someone older and wiser has something to teach us. Even when we know a lot of things, there is always something to learn. Respecting our elders by hearing them is one way to please the Lord.

Look up this memory verse and say it out loud: Luke 2:52
"And Jesus grew in wisdom and stature and in favor with God and man."

Pray about it: Thank God for the things He teaches us. Ask Him to help you be obedient and listen this week.

Active time!
The Bible says that Jesus grew in wisdom and stature. That means He understood more as He grew taller, stronger, and older! Look at pictures of yourself when you were younger. How have you grown physically? What things do you understand now that you're older? Now, write down your current age, height, weight, grade in school, the last book you read, and anything else that can measure your size and understanding. Keep this in a safe place until next year, then see how much you've grown!

Bonus fun: Practice listening to an elder by asking someone older than you to tell you a story about when they were a kid. To do a little extra, try to write their story and/or illustrate it, then give it to them as a gift.

My Time With God:

Parable of the Sower

The Scripture: Matthew 13:1-23

Stories are a fun way for us to learn. Jesus knew that stories help people understand the ways of God, so He told what we call "parables." A parable is a story with a lesson. The parable of the sower (someone who plants things) was especially helpful to the people listening to Jesus, because they were farmers. Jesus knew they would understand a little better if he used a symbol of something familiar, like planting seeds.

His story was about a farmer who planted seeds. Some seed fell on the hard path and was eaten by birds. Some of it ended up in rocky places where the dirt was shallow. It grew quickly and died because the roots couldn't go deep enough. Some of the seeds were planted among thorns. When those plants grew, the thorns choked them out. But finally, there were seeds that landed in good soil. These plants grew and produced more plants!

Jesus wanted to teach about something that was hard to see- God's kingdom and our hearts. So He turned something that was easy to see (seeds and plants) into symbols. It was still difficult to understand, but He lovingly took the time to explain it to the disciples. The seeds represented people. People react differently when they hear the Word of God. Some people don't care and ignore it. Other people are so distracted by sin that good news about Jesus doesn't stay in their hearts. Sometimes, people have joy for a short time, then get tired of following God and start to live their own way as soon as life gets hard. There are people who care more about their worries or being rich than about God's Word. But there are many people who hear the gospel, understand it, keep it in their hearts, and follow God. That's the kind of person we want to be.

Can you match up the kind of people with the types of seeds? Now you understand one of Jesus' parables!

Look up this memory verse and say it out loud: Matthew 13:23a "But the seed falling on good soil refers to someone who hears the word and understands it. "

Pray about it: Thank God for the things He teaches us. Ask Him to show you something new about Himself this week.

Active time!

Be a sower! Plant seeds in pots with soils similar to what Jesus described in the story. Label them like the hearts in the parable, water them, and watch how they grow.

Pot 1- Hard dirt with bird seed on top. Place outside where birds can find it.

Pot 2- Soil mixed with lots of rocks. Place in a very sunny spot.

Pot 3- Plant along with weeds or a bigger plant. Watch to see if your little seeds survive.

Pot 4- Plant these seeds with a rose. Watch out for thorns! (If you don't have a rose, you can label Pot 3 with this soil, too.)

Pot 5- Use good soil, place in just the right amount of sunlight, and be sure to give your plants plenty of water.

Bonus fun: Be a scientist explorer. Go outside and find plants where they are growing. Note the type of plant, soil conditions, how much sunlight they get, and draw pictures. What conclusions do you find about plant types and how they grow?

My Time With God:

Parable of the Good Samaritan

The Scripture: Luke 10:25–37

It can be difficult to study God's Word sometimes. Jesus knew that some ideas are hard to learn, so He told stories to help His disciples understand. These made-up parables were not actual events, but they are still important to remember. We can learn a lot from Jesus' stories.

This parable is about a man who was traveling, but he was caught by robbers and beaten. While he was laying on the side of the road, a priest walked by and ignored him. Then, Levite (someone who worked in the temple), walked by and ignored the man, too. Then, a Samaritan man came by. This person was kind and helped the hurt man. He cared for his injuries, then took him to a place where he could rest and heal. At the end of this story, Jesus asked, "Who was a good neighbor?"

Jesus told the parable of the Good Samaritan to help the people understand that it's important to love our neighbor no matter what. In the time Jesus lived, many Jewish people didn't like anyone from a placed called Samaria (those people were called Samaritans). But in Jesus' story, the Samaritan was the person who followed God's way the most. Jesus wanted everyone to know that every person is our neighbor, no matter where they live or if they are different than us. This is because we are all God's children.

Did you learn anything else from the parable of the Good Samaritan? What does this parable teach us about how to treat people who are different than we are?

Look up this memory verse and say it out loud: Luke 10:27 "'Love the Lord your God with all your heart and with all your soul and with all your strength and with all your mind'; and, 'Love your neighbor as yourself.'"

Pray about it: Thank God for His teaching stories. Ask Him to show you something new about the Good Samaritan and help you be a good neighbor.

Active time!
Stop and think about the people around you who are different than you. Do you know anyone at school, church, or in your community that is from a different place? Follows a different religion? Has another skin color or lives with a disability? What other things make us different?
Instead of letting differences keep you apart, do something to be closer to a new friend. What can you do to share God's love with your neighbor? Don't just sit there, go do it!

Bonus fun: The Good Samaritan was a helper in a dangerous situation. Talk to your family and make a disaster plan in case of emergency. Know what to do in case of a fire, flood, tornado, or earthquake. You can also assemble a first aid kit for sickness or injuries. What items would you include? There is no reason to be scared of emergencies because God is always with you. Being prepared keeps everyone safe!

My Time With God:

Kids in the Bible

The Scripture: Matthew 14:13-21

We've met some great kids in our journey so far, like Samuel, who heard God's voice… or David, who fought a giant! We even got to see what Jesus was like when He was young. Now we learn about a kid who got to be part of a miracle.

Jesus was teaching for a long time on a day when many people came to listen. There were 5,000 men plus all the women and children! After such a long day, everyone was hungry. But they were far from a place that could provide enough food for everyone. The disciples asked everyone in the crowd if they brought food, but the only person who had anything was a young boy! He had packed a lunch of two fishes and five loaves of bread. Jesus took that lunch, thanked God, and then did a miracle- he turned the boy's lunch into enough food to feed all of those people! The boy in this story of fishes and loaves is just one more kid who got to do big things thanks to God.

How many times has a grown-up asked you what you want to be when you grow up? What do you usually tell them? Now, has anyone asked you what you want to be today? What you'd like to do tomorrow?

It's great fun to dream about the future. Having goals for the future helps us make good decisions now. But we don't have to wait to be an adult to do amazing things for the Lord. Just like the kids in the Bible, God can use us for His kingdom today. All we have to do is be willing, obedient, and ready when He calls.

Look up this memory verse and say it out loud: 1 Timothy 4:12 "Don't let anyone look down on you because you are young, but set an example for the believers in speech, in conduct, in love, in faith and in purity."

Pray about it: Thank God for the honor of serving Him. Ask God to show you what He has planned for you today and this week.

Active time!
What do you think it was like to be a kid in the Bible? How did kids spend their time without television, video games, or extra-curricular activities? Ask a parent, head to the library, or search the internet to find out what life was like in Bible times, especially for kids.

Bonus fun: Play an ancient kid game! Have you heard of the game mancala? It's an old game that we still play today. Jesus may have even played it! Also, learn how to spin a dreidel or do cat's cradle with some string. You can even invent your own game with marbles or stones and drawing things in the dirt. All of these are ways kids in Bible times probably played together.

<u>My Time With God:</u>

Love Your Enemies

The Scripture: Matthew 5:38-48

The word "conflict" means a disagreement, argument, or a fight. Have you ever had conflict with a friend, brother, or sister?

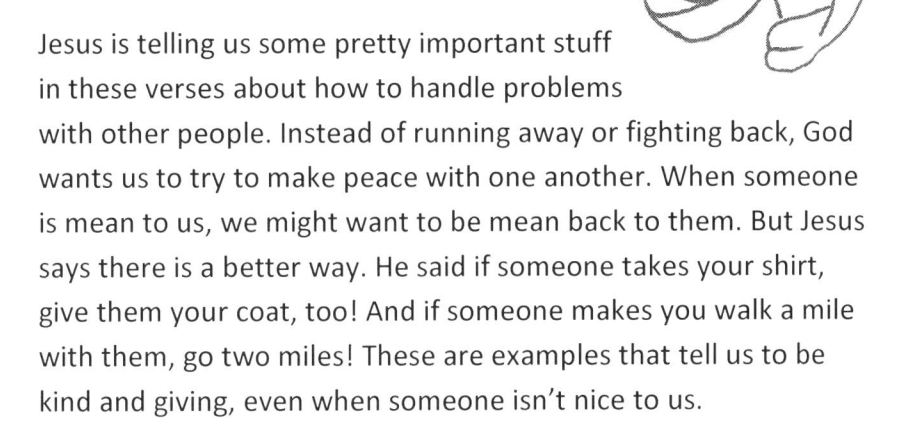

Jesus is telling us some pretty important stuff in these verses about how to handle problems with other people. Instead of running away or fighting back, God wants us to try to make peace with one another. When someone is mean to us, we might want to be mean back to them. But Jesus says there is a better way. He said if someone takes your shirt, give them your coat, too! And if someone makes you walk a mile with them, go two miles! These are examples that tell us to be kind and giving, even when someone isn't nice to us.

It's not always easy to do what Jesus describes here, but it IS possible. Jesus says to love our enemies and pray for those who are mean to us. And when that's done, the results are worth the effort. Our enemies can become our friends!

Was there a time you were nice to someone who was mean to you? What happened?

Can you think of ways to love someone who isn't acting loving to you right now?

Look up this memory verse and say it out loud: Matthew 38:44-45
"Love your enemies and pray for those who persecute you, that you may be children of your God in heaven."

Pray about it: Thank God for loving us all the time. Ask Him to help us love *everyone* the way He loves all people.

Active time!

Have a movie night! Check out the VeggieTales "Are You My Neighbor," or perhaps "How to Train Your Dragon" for older kids. What do these movies show about loving enemies? Can you think of any other movies, television shows, or books you know that practice the scripture we just learned? Make a snack and enjoy!

Bonus fun: The Bible says that it's not enough to only read the scripture and hear the Word of God. We need to practice what Jesus is telling us to do. Now that you know that God definitely wants you to love your enemy, how can you do that? It may be very difficult, so make sure to pray about it and maybe even talk to a parent or teacher for guidance. Maybe you need to forgive someone so that you can love them. Take action today to share God's love with someone who has hurt you. You can do it!

<u>My Time With God:</u>

Jesus the Carpenter

The Scripture: Matthew 13:53-58

Sometimes we need to pay close attention to learn something about Jesus. With a little detective work, we learn that Jesus was a carpenter!

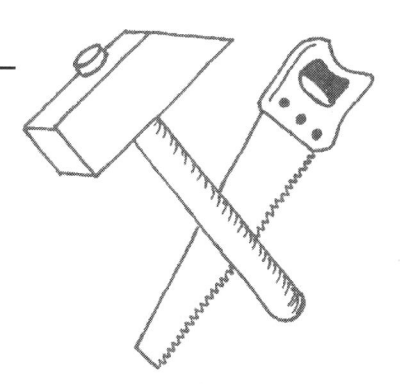

From the stories of His birth, we discovered that Jesus' mother was Mary and His father on earth was Joseph. Now, fast forward to when Jesus was an adult. He traveled to heal, teach, and share God's love with the people. Most of the people were very glad to see Him. One day, he returned to His hometown of Nazareth. Things were different there.

Unlike the other towns He visited, the people in Nazareth didn't believe in Jesus. They only remembered watching Him grow up and didn't see anything special about Him. They only saw Him as "the carpenter's son"- an ordinary person.

This is a big clue about how Jesus grew! In those times, kids learned the skills of their parents. If Joseph was a carpenter, Jesus would be a carpenter, too. As soon as He was old enough, He would've worked next to Joseph, who taught Jesus everything he knew about building things. What do you imagine that Jesus built?

Our families are a special gift from God. There are many things we can learn from our parents. What can your family teach you?

Look up this memory verse and say it out loud: Deuteronomy 5:16
"Honor your father and your mother, as the Lord your God has commanded you, so that you may live long and that it may go well with you in the land the Lord your God is giving you."

Pray about it: Thank God for giving us our family. Ask Him to show you what you can learn from your parents.

Active time!
Make a wood project like Jesus the carpenter. Many craft stores have easy-to-make kits, or you can be creative with supplies you have at home, like craft sticks and glue. Make sure you ask an adult for help to stay safe if you want to try something complicated.

Bonus fun: Learn a new skill from a parent, older relative, or neighbor. Try something you've always wanted to do or be surprised when they teach you something very new and different. They will be delighted to spend time with you as well, so you will both be blessed by this project.

My Time With God:

Fishing for People

The Scripture: Luke 5:1-11; 6:12-16

Did you know Jesus had friends? His followers traveled with Him, listened to His stories and teaching, and even laughed and cried with Jesus. Here's how they met:

Jesus was walking beside the Sea of Galilee and saw two men fishing. Their names were Peter and Andrew. They had been fishing all night, but did not catch anything. Jesus told them to put their nets out in the deep water. They did, and caught so many fish their nets almost broke! Jesus said, "Come with me and I will teach you how to fish for people!" So Peter and Andrew went with Him. Then, they saw two other fishermen named James and John. Jesus invited them to come, too!

When Jesus asked the disciples to follow Him, it meant that they had to give up the things they usually did every day. The fishermen would stop spending their days on the water, catching and selling fish to provide for themselves and their families. Levi had to stop collecting taxes, a job that made lots of money. Now, the men had to trust that Jesus would take care of everything they needed.

When God asks us to change, sometimes the only thing we see is what we're going to lose. The disciples took a big risk by leaving their jobs. But, they also lost some problems. They didn't have to worry about days when they didn't catch many fish. They also didn't have to worry about trying to work through storms and bad weather or fixing their boats when something broke. When they traveled with Jesus, these were no longer troublesome. What a good thing to lose!

When Jesus filled the fishermen's nets with fish, He showed them that He would make sure they had everything they needed. Instead of worrying about what they would lose by following Jesus, the disciples saw what they would gain. They now had the peace of trusting God and the many blessings to follow.

Look up this memory verse and say it out loud: Mark 1:17 "Jesus said to them, 'Follow me, and I will make you fishers of men.'"

Pray about it: Thank God for showing you the way through life. Ask God to help you trust and follow Him.

Active time!
When God wants to teach us something, He usually begins with something we already know. When Jesus invited the disciples to follow Him, He explained what they would do next. To make it easy for them to understand, Jesus used an example of something they already knew a lot about- fishing. But instead of gathering fish, now they would help Jesus gather people into God's kingdom! To help remember this, if you know how to fish, ask to go on a fishing trip! You can also make your own fishing game with magnets, paper clips, string, and paper fish. See how many you can gather.

Bonus fun: Play a fishy game! Find a deck of cards and play "Go Fish." The object of the game is to collect as many matched cards as possible. Each player starts with seven cards in their hand, and the rest of the cards in a pile face down between them. One player chooses another player and asks if they have a certain card that matches one in their hand. If the other player has it, they give it to the asking player. If not, they say, "go fish" and the asking player gets to draw from the pile in the middle. Take turns until the cards are gone. The person with the most matches is the winner!

My Time With God:

Zaccaheus

The Scripture: Luke 19:1-10

Have you ever felt like you weren't good enough? Not smart enough? Not talented enough? Zacchaeus felt that way. He wasn't tall enough.

Jesus was coming to town and everyone crowded around the street to see Him. But Zacchaeus, a local tax collector, was too short to see over everyone. He was afraid he would miss seeing Jesus.

Zacchaeus could've given up right away. But he wanted to see Jesus so much that he came up with a plan. Climbing a tree would give him a better view than anyone else!

His plan worked. Not only did he see Jesus, but Jesus saw him. And then He went to Zacchaeus' house for dinner!

Jesus didn't care how tall Zacchaeus was. He didn't ignore Zacchaeus because of the way he acted as a dishonest tax collector. Jesus loved him just the way he was. In fact, He loved Zacchaeus so much that He helped Zacchaeus grow! No, Jesus did not make him taller, but He helped Zacchaeus grow on the inside by changing his heart. Now Zacchaeus would follow God and treat people with love.

When you feel like you aren't enough, remember Zacchaeus. Remember that Jesus loves you exactly the way you are, and He is going to help you keep growing. What do you think you'll become with Jesus?

Look up this memory verse and say it out loud: Luke 19:10 "For the Son of Man came to seek and to save the lost."

Pray about it: Thank God for the way He made you. Ask God to help you follow Him and keep growing closer to Him.

Active time!

Have you ever climbed a tree? With a parent's permission and supervision, try to climb a tree in your backyard or neighborhood. Imagine what it was like for Zacchaeus to try to reach the branches and pull himself up high enough to see over the crowd. If you don't have a safe tree, head over to the local playground. Use your imagination as you climb the play structures at the park!

Bonus fun: Measure how you grow. Take a measurement of your height and mark it on a piece of paper. Also, trace around your hand and foot. Keep these in a safe place or give it to a parent. Then, mark on a calendar to check them in six months, then again in a year, and even after that to see how much you are growing. If you were with Zacchaeus, do you think you could see over the crowd, or would you need to join him in the tree?

My Time With God:

Jesus Heals the Blind

The Scripture: Mark 8:22-26, 10:46-52

As Jesus traveled and taught about the Kingdom of God, He also healed many people. The book of Mark shares a couple of stories about how Jesus healed blind men. These particular men had very different stories.

A blind man at Bethsaida had good friends, and those friends took the man to Jesus. Jesus touched the man's eyes, and he could see! After he was healed, the man was sent home.

Another time, a blind man named Bartimaeus was sitting by the side of the road. Unlike the other blind man, he did not have friends. He was all alone. But Bartimaeus believed that Jesus could heal him. So when Jesus came down the road, Bartimaeus began calling out for Him. The crowd around him that told him to be quiet! But Jesus heard his cries and healed him. This time was different than the othe blind man, because Jesus didn't have to touch Bartimaeus to heal him. And after he was healed, Bartimaeus didn't go home- he followed Jesus.

Why do you think these stories are so different? Could it be because the two men were very different people? We don't get many details about the lives of the blind men, but we do know that God makes every person unique. But no matter how different we are, Jesus loves us the same! Even though the men had different stories, they were both healed and were able to see.

Look up this memory verse and say it out loud: Mark 10:52
"'Go,' said Jesus, 'your faith has healed you.'"

Pray about it: Thank God for healing us when we are sick. Ask God to help you see His ways clearly.

Active time!
Optical illusions can be fun! Find a book at the library or get permission to search the internet to find optical illusions. See how pictures can play tricks on our vision.

Bonus fun: Have you ever taken an eye test? You can make your own at home. Use your computer to write down some words or even just a bunch of letters. Make the letters as big as you can on the top row, then a little smaller as each row goes down the page. Print out your eye test and hang it on the wall. Step back about ten steps, and see how far down you can read clearly before the letters become blurry. Then, cover one eye and test your open eye. Next, cover the other eye and see which one is stronger.

My Time With God:

Mary and Martha

The Scripture: Luke 10:38-42

What do you think it was like to be Jesus' friend? Mary and Martha may not have traveled with Him like the disciples, but He often came to visit them when He was in their town. If you knew Jesus was coming over to your house, how would you get ready for Him?

Both Mary and Martha loved Jesus very much, and they were both doing their best to treat their guest well. But Martha didn't have a very good attitude. She was cooking and cleaning, but her sister Mary was not helping! Instead, she was sitting at Jesus' feet and listening to him talk. Martha was mad at Mary, then tried to get Jesus to take her side. That's not a very good way to treat a guest at all. It's also not a good way to treat a close friend.

Jesus told Martha that Mary chose the better way by sitting and listening to Him. Martha tried to do something nice for Jesus, but she didn't have love in her heart. Jesus probably didn't get to visit very often. But Martha didn't think of spending as much time with Him as possible. Instead, she was worried about making sure her house was nice. Jesus wanted her to make Him the most important thing.

Is loving Jesus the most important thing to you? When you go to church or do your Bible time, are you distracted by the busy activities? It's easy to spend too much time on other good things and forget to think about Jesus! We must keep love in our hearts and our eyes on Jesus all the time.

Look up this memory verse and say it out loud: 1 Corinthians 13:2b
"If I have a faith that can move mountains, but do not have love, I am nothing."

Pray about it: Thank God for being part of your life. Ask God to help you keep your eyes on Jesus no matter what you are doing.

Active time!
Clean house like Martha, but do it with love in your heart. You can help your family by doing something to clean your home. Be sure to do it cheerfully and with happiness while you're helping.

Bonus fun: Listen to Jesus like Mary. You can enjoy praise and worship music or read an extra chapter or story in your Bible. Be sure to talk to Him in prayer, too!

<u>My Time With God:</u>

Parable of the Talents

The Scripture: Matthew 25:14–30

To understand this story, we need to learn a little bit about life during Bible times. "Talent" meant something different than it does now. In this story, a "talent" is a measurement of how much something weighed. It tells us how much gold the master gave his servants. Historical records say that a talent was around 75-110 pounds. That's about the same weight as a person! Can you think of anything else that weighs that much? Or how many smaller things would weigh that much together?

Now imagine having 75 pounds of gold. That's as much as an average ten-year-old! Then think of five different piles of that gold. That's how much a master gave his first servant. That's quite a treasure! You can imagine two piles of gold for the second servant, and one pile for the third one. After the master gave his servants the gold, he went on a trip. The first two servants were very wise with the master's money. They did things to earn more gold, like possibly spending the money to make a business that earned more money. What else could they have done to increase their supply of gold?

The third servant was worried about keeping the money safe, so he hid it where no one would find it until it was time to give it back to the master. When the master returned, he was very happy with the first two servants! But when he found out the third servant buried the money, the master was frustrated. Even if the servant only wanted to keep it safe, he could've saved it in a bank and earned interest, which is money the bank gives someone who keeps money there.

What do you think God wants us to learn from this? If talents are something God gives us, then they can be anything from money or things, love and caring, or even gifts and abilities. What do we do with them? If we share them, they grow, and God gives us more. But if we keep them to ourselves, it doesn't help anyone. Do you think that makes God very happy?

What has God given you? And what are you doing with these things?

Look up this memory verse and say it out loud: Luke 16:10 "Whoever can be trusted with very little can also be trusted with much, and whoever is dishonest with very little will also be dishonest with much."

Pray about it: Thank God for giving us gifts. Ask God how you can use those gifts this week.

Active time!

Write down all the gifts God has given your family. Now decide what you will do with those gifts this week. Then work together to make your plan happen!

Bonus fun: Host a talent show! Gather friends and family, then give everyone a chance to showcase their special gifts. You might even serve a special snack or act as emcee or host. Don't forget to give lots of encouraging applause!

<u>My Time With God:</u>

Jesus Raises Lazarus

The Scripture: John 11:1-44

Do you remember Jesus' friends, Mary and Martha? They also had a brother named Lazarus. Jesus loved these three very much.

Lazarus got very sick one day. Jesus was not nearby, but when He heard the news, He told the disciples that it would be ok. Lazarus' sickness would not end in death, and everything would happen for God's glory. He did not hurry to go back to Lazarus' town. A few days later, they got sad news that Lazarus had died. That's when Jesus went back to his friends Mary and Martha.

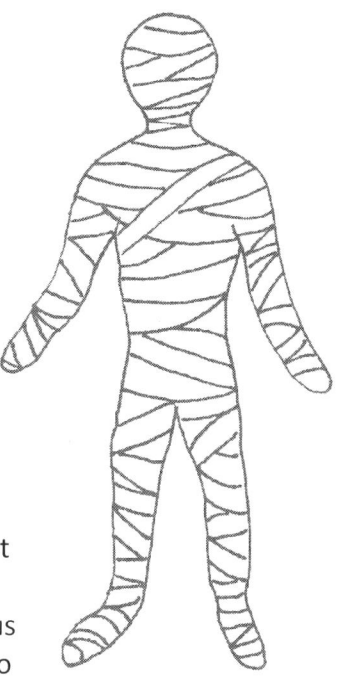

When we love someone, we are happy when they are happy, and sad when they are sad. Jesus was the same way. The Bible says "Jesus wept" when he visited Lazarus' grave and saw how upset Mary and Martha were. That means he cried very much and with a lot of sadness.

While Jesus was weeping, the people questioned why He didn't come sooner and heal His friend. The answer to this is in the very beginning of our story. Remember, Jesus told the disciples that Lazarus' sickness "would not end in death," but that it was for God's glory. And that's exactly what happened! Jesus raised Lazarus from the dead, all the people saw the glory of God! Then, they believed that Jesus was sent by God.

Sometimes, bad things happen to us. That doesn't mean that God doesn't love us or that He's not taking care of us. God is always with us and loves us very much. When bad things happen, we need to remember that He is in charge. We have to wait to see how our story will end before we give up hope. God works out everything to show us His glory.

Look up this memory verse and say it out loud: Romans 8:28 "We know that in all things God works for the good of those who love Him, who have been called according to His purpose."

Pray about it: Thank God for always taking care of you. Ask God to help you trust Him and to show you His glory in all situations.

Active time!

After Lazarus died, he was wrapped up in strips of linen and put in a grave- likely a small cave. Ask a sibling or a buddy to play a game. Using a roll of toilet paper, one person wraps the other up like a mummy, as tight as they can. When they are done, say "Lazarus, come forth!" The wrapped person tries to get out of the wrap as quickly as they can. Then, switch and see who was the fastest at escaping.

Bonus fun: Make up a story about someone who was having a bad day, but Jesus changed that. You can set it in any time period with any characters. Write your story down on paper or tell it someone else.

My Time With God:

Jesus and the Tax Collector

The Scripture: Mark 2:13-17

Tax collectors were not popular guys. People didn't like to have their hard-earned money taken away. Taxes were often very high, leaving little money for the people to keep. To make things worse, tax collectors usually charged extra to keep for themselves or used other ways to cheat the people out of their money. Tax collectors did not honor God's law that said not to steal or lie.

Imagine how surprised God's people were to find Jesus at a dinner party full of tax collectors! They thought that God's Son should only spend time with people who were good. They didn't realize what Jesus knew- that even tax collectors can change and follow God.

Jesus said that He came for sinners, which means people who don't live God's way all the time. That means everyone, because nobody is perfect except Jesus! He loves everyone, even people who make bad decisions. God can change the heart of any person into one who loves and follows Him, if only that person is willing.

Oh, and as for Levi the tax collector? He was willing to love God and become a follower of Jesus. You might know him by his other name: Matthew the disciple.

Look up this memory verse and say it out loud: Mark 2:17
"Jesus said to them, "It is not the healthy who need a doctor, but the sick. I have not come to call the righteous, but sinners.""

Pray about it: Thank God for loving you even when you sin. Ask God to help you see other people the way He sees them.

Active time!

Do you have the game Monopoly? Play it with a family member or friend, and be like a tax collector in charge of the money. Make sure you are a good and honest tax collector!

Bonus fun: A good tax collector needed excellent math skills. Find a workbook, a math game online or on a phone app, or ask an adult to give you some practice problems so you can sharpen your own numbers skills!

My Time With God:

The Wise Man and the Foolish Man

The Scripture: Matthew 7:24-29

In this story, Jesus uses symbolism to help people understand His message. He wants everyone to know that God's Word is the best foundation for our life.

There was a wise man who built his house on rock and a foolish man who built his house on the sand. When rain and wind came, the house that was built on the rock stood safe and sound. But the house on the sand fell down and smashed!

When you build a house, you start at the bottom. You want to make sure that the bottom of the house is strong and secure on the ground. If it moves, the whole house will come down! Jesus said our lives are similar. We need to start with the wisdom of God's Word so that we'll know how to make good decisions and follow Christ.

Jesus wants us to listen to His words and then practice doing what He says. If we do that, we will make good decisions, avoid sin, and glorify God. But, He says if we hear His words but don't practice them, we will be like the foolish man. We will make bad decisions, we'll sin, and it will not please God. It will feel like our life is falling apart like the foolish man's house!

You get to choose if you will practice Jesus' teachings or not. Will you be wise or foolish?

Look up this memory verse and say it out loud: Matthew 7:24 "Everyone who hears these words of mine and puts them into practice is like a wise man who built his house on the rock."

Pray about it: Thank God for teaching us to be wise. Ask God to help you learn His Word and make good decisions.

Active time!
Build a block tower or stack books on a sturdy surface, like a table or hard floor. Then try stacking them on a soft surface, like a pillow or blanket. Which tower is stronger? How is this like the story Jesus told?

Bonus fun: Learn how to build a house of cards! Start by leaning two cards against each other until they balance and stand on their own. Then slowly start to add cards around them, being very careful to balance and not knock anything over. Find some helpful hints at www.bedtimemath.org/how-to-build-a-house-of-cards/.

My Time With God:

Jesus Heals a Deaf Man

The Scripture: Mark 7:31-37

Jesus healed many people as he traveled and taught. He met people with all kinds of problems and illnesses. In this story, Jesus healed a man who could not hear and could barely speak.

This healing might seem strange. Some people brought a man who could not hear or speak to Jesus. Jesus put his fingers in the man's ears, then spit and touched the man's tongue. Then He looked to heaven and said, "Be opened!" And then the man was healed and could hear and talk!

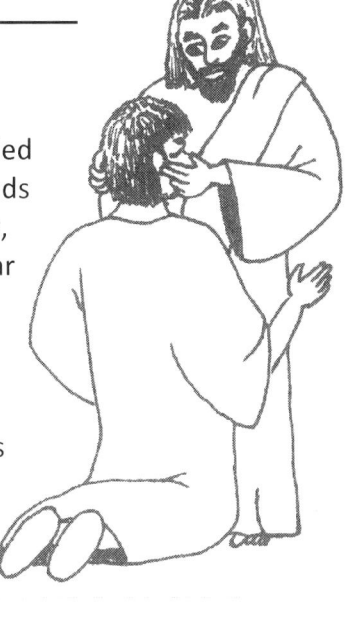

Just like when he healed the blind man at Bethsaida, Jesus spit when he healed the man who could not hear. Why do you think He did this?

The Bible doesn't tell us why, but we can make some guesses. At that time and in that place, many people thought spit, or saliva, could be part of healing. Some teachers think maybe Jesus made some mud out of the dust and used that as part of His work. Others say that his saliva was a symbol and that it was like when Jesus gave His blood on the cross when He forgave our sins. These are all interesting ideas.

We may not know why Jesus spit when He healed the deaf man, but we do know that Jesus didn't need to do any tricks to make people well. He is the Son of God who loves us and is powerful enough to heal any sickness or pain. The important part of the story is that the deaf man could hear and that people were amazed at the power of God!

Look up this memory verse and say it out loud: Psalm 30:2 "Lord my God, I called to you for help, and you healed me."

Pray about it: Thank God for His healing power. Ask God to help you understand His ways a little bit more each day.

Active time!

Close your eyes and listen to music. Then, turn off the music and just listen to the noises around you. What do you hear the longer you listen? Do any sounds surprise you? Do you ever forget to be thankful for the sense of hearing?

Bonus fun: Use earmuffs or a scarf to cover your ears. For thirty minutes, see what it's like to experience life without hearing. What did you discover?

My Time With God:

The Lord's Prayer

The Scripture: Matthew 6:9-13, 1 Thessalonians 5:17

Let's talk about prayer. Prayer simply means a conversation with God. You don't have to use big, fancy words or be at church to talk to God. Talking to the Lord is just like talking to a friend! And since God is always with us, we can pray at any time and in any place.

Jesus taught the disciples to pray in two ways. First, Jesus was a good example. He prayed to God, too! Then, one day, Jesus sat on mountainside and taught the disciples many things. This included what we now call "The Lord's Prayer." Did you read it yet? If not, open your Bible to Matthew 6:9-13 and check it out now.

We can pray the prayer exactly like it is written in the Bible, or we can use it as a guide to remind us the many parts of prayer. These are things like thankfulness, praising God, asking for things we need, asking for forgiveness, and for God to protect us from temptation.

Many churches say the Lord's Prayer together every Sunday. Church tradition added one more line to the end: "For Thine is the kingdom, and the power, and the glory forever. Amen." Does your church say the Lord's Prayer? Do you have it memorized already?

In 1 Thessalonians, Paul says, "Pray without ceasing." He means that prayer should be a regular, frequent habit. How do you think your "prayer habit" is doing? How can you help your prayer life grow?

Look up this memory verse and say it out loud: Matthew 6:9b-10 "Our Father in heaven, hallowed be Your name, Your kingdom come, Your will be done, on earth as it is in heaven."
Pray about it: Practice saying the Lord's Prayer until you know it by heart.

Active time!
Pray out loud. Find a place where only God can hear you. Some people pray in a closet. Other people like to go outside and be in nature. Maybe you can even pray when you take a shower and the water is running! However you feel comfortable, talk to God the same way you talk to a friend. Tell Him everything that's on your mind. When you're done, sit quietly for as long as you can to rest in His presence.

Bonus fun: Make a Lord's Prayer mix-up game. Write each word of the prayer on a separate card or piece of paper. Then, shuffle the cards and mix them well. Now, start a timer and see how quickly you can put the words of the Lord's Prayer in order. If you make two sets, you can race a friend!

My Time With God:

Flowers and Sparrows

The Scripture: Matthew 6:25-30

What do you worry about? Are you scared of anything?

The disciples and followers of Jesus had worries, too. So, Jesus helped them understand how God takes care of us. First, He pointed out the birds. He reminded the disciples that God takes care of them. What animals would Jesus use to remind you how much God cares? You are more important to God than even the biggest, most special animal on the planet!

Sometimes, we won't stop worrying, so Jesus keeps teaching us until we understand. He was on a mountainside when he was teaching the disciples, so he looked around and pointed at the wildflowers growing all around them. Who takes care of the flowers in the wilderness, in fields, or on mountains? No people water them or pull the weeds around them. But God takes care of His beautiful creation.

And guess what? He loves His children more than anything else He created in the whole universe! Wow! How incredible! Jesus wants us to know that we never have to worry, because God will always take care of everything we need. We are so important to Him that He will never let us go.

Look up this memory verse and say it out loud: Philippians 4:19 "God will meet all your needs according to the riches of His glory in Christ Jesus."

Pray about it: Thank God for taking such good care of you. Ask God to help you trust Him instead of worrying.

Active time!
To understand how God takes care of flowers, plant some flowers of your own. Make sure they get the right amount of sun and water. What happens if you miss a day of care? How is taking care of flowers similar to the way God takes care of us?

Bonus fun: We can help God care for the birds by making a bird feeder. If you have hummingbirds, all it takes is sugar water to make them happy. Another simple bird-feeding creation is to spread peanut butter all over a pinecone, then roll it in birdseed. Tie a string around it and hang it outside for a bird treat (but don't do this if you are allergic to peanut butter)! There are many ways to make birdfeeders, even scattering seeds on the ground. How does God provide for us the way He takes care of birds?

My Time With God:

Triumphal Entry

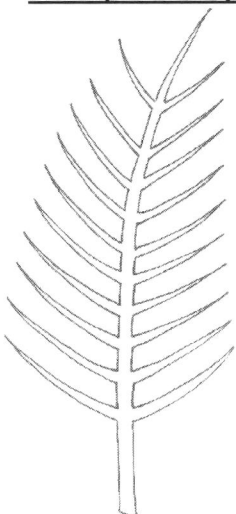

The Scripture: Mark 11:1-11

When someone special comes to visit, we prepare and then welcome them. We want them to know how glad we are that they arrived and how much we enjoy spending time with them. What are some things your family does to welcome someone to your home?

The people of Jerusalem welcomed Jesus with a celebration. As he rode into town on a donkey, the threw their coats on the ground in front of him. Then they waved palm branches and shouted, "Hosanna! Blessed is He who comes in the name of the Lord!" The people showed Jesus that they were glad to see Him and that they knew who He was. Other people saw the excitement and soon learned about Jesus, as well. Of course, not everyone welcomed Him. Many of the priests in the temple were not so happy to see Him, because they didn't like some of the things Jesus taught.

We have the chance to welcome Jesus into our lives, too. Is He part of your daily routine? How can someone tell that Jesus is welcome in your house or with your family? What do you do to invite Jesus to come in?

Look up this memory verse and say it out loud: Mark 1:4
"Hosanna! Blessed is He who comes in the name of the Lord!"

Pray about it: Thank God for coming to us and being in our lives. Ask God to help you see Him and welcome Him, too!

Active time!
Unless you happen to have a horse, go outside and ride your bike. What do you think Jesus saw when He rode the donkey through the crowd? Why do you think he rode instead of walked?

Bonus fun: Create signs or a banner to welcome Jesus. Use your imagination to make them as colorful as possible. When you're done, hang them somewhere in your home as a reminder that Jesus is not only welcome, but that you're excited that He's in your life. Maybe you can lead a parade through your house or neighborhood that praises the Lord!

My Time With God:

Jesus Dies on the Cross

The Scripture: Mark 14-15

What is your favorite story about Jesus? Do you like to hear about when He was born and when He was a boy in the temple? What about the times He spent with His disciples? Maybe you like to hear about miracles again and again. There are so many good stories about Jesus.

The story of Jesus on the cross is very sad. After celebrating the Passover dinner with His disciples, Jesus went to a garden to pray. While He was there, a mob came and arrested Him. Jesus spent the night on trial, and finally was taken to an official named Pilate. Pilate tried to let Jesus go, but there were many people who didn't like Jesus yelling "Crucify Him!" That means they wanted to kill Jesus by hanging Him on a cross.

Soldiers hurt Jesus and tore His clothes. Jesus was in a lot of pain. His friends left Him. He was punished and beaten. The government leaders and temple teachers were not being fair. They nailed Jesus to a cross and put Him on a hill with two criminals. On that cross, Jesus died.

Does this part of the story make you want to cry? Does it make you angry? How would you feel if you were a follower of Jesus during this dark time?

The story of Jesus on the cross is also beautiful, because it is a story of love. God loves all His children, including you! He wants His children (including you) to be with Him forever in heaven. But there's a problem- there is no sin allowed in heaven. And all God's children have sinned. Sin keeps people far from God! There was only one answer.

Someone had to take the punishment for all the sins of all the people. And that someone had to be perfect and never have sinned at all. There was only one possibility- God's very own Son, Jesus. If He died on the cross, He would take over the punishment for all the sins of all the people in the entire world- even those born generations later! Then, all the people who love God could be with Him forever.

Jesus could have escaped the punishment at any time. Instead, He stayed and died on the cross because He loves us all so much. That's a beautiful story, and it's not over yet.

Look up this memory verse and say it out loud: 1 Thessalonians 5:1
"He died for us so that, whether we are awake or asleep, we may live together with him."

Pray about it: Thank God for sending Jesus to earth to die for us. Take some time to tell Him sorry for the things you've done wrong and thank Him for His loving forgiveness.

Active time!
Make a cross to remember how Jesus died. You can make it out of any material you'd like and any size you want. Put your cross in a place you will see it often.

Bonus fun: The story of Jesus on the cross has a lot to think about. Ask a grown-up if you can go on a walk. You can talk about the story or just think about it quietly. Moving our legs and getting fresh air helps us think and process big thoughts.

<u>**My Time With God:**</u>

Christis Risen!

The Scripture: Matthew 28

After Jesus died on the cross, He was buried in a tomb with a big rock to cover the entrance. His followers were very sad and hiding from all the people who didn't like Jesus. One morning, a few days after Jesus had died, some women who loved Him went to the tomb. What they found was very surprising.

The big stone that covered the tomb had been rolled away! The tomb was empty! And then they saw an angel. The angel told them not to be afraid and that Jesus was alive!!

Jesus Christ is risen! How exciting! He died on the cross, but he didn't stay dead! Instead, Jesus resurrected- or came back to life- and got to spend more time with his disciples and friends. Can you imagine how incredible what was? How do you think the disciples felt after being so sad, then discovering that Jesus was alive?

We share their excitement when we celebrate Easter every year. We sing songs full of joy and remember the happy story. We eat special food (like chocolate bunnies!), play festive games (like egg hunts!), and spend time with our family. Then we go to bed, wake up the next morning, then.... what?

I bet the disciples wondered the same thing. After the surprise wore off, what did they do next? No one else had ever done what Jesus did, and nothing would ever be the same as it was before. Check out the end of our scripture, where Jesus tells them (and us) exactly what to do next.

But wait! Jesus' story is not over yet! Even when we've turned the last page in the Bible, our story with God keeps going. We don't stop celebrating the Resurrection after Easter Sunday. Every day of our lives can be a celebration of our risen Lord.

Knowing how much God loves us makes a difference in everything we do. We have hope and joy knowing that we'll be with Jesus in heaven someday. It's easier to forgive other people when we know how God forgave us. And we have so much of God's love to share with everyone we meet! Read verses 18-20 out loud again, and think about how you'll follow these instructions and celebrate Jesus every day.

Look up this memory verse and say it out loud: Matthew 28:19-20
"Therefore go and make disciples of all nations, baptizing them in the name of the Father and of the Son and of the Holy Spirit, and teaching them to obey everything I have commanded you. And surely I am with you always, to the very end of the age."

Pray about it: Thank God that He is alive and always with us! Ask Him to help you live so everyone knows that Jesus has risen!

Active time!
Decorate your house for Easter, no matter what season it is right now. If you don't have Easter decorations, you can easily make some! Be sure to include something that says "Christ is Risen" as you remember the reason for the celebration!

Bonus fun: Planting seeds can remind us of Jesus' resurrection. Have an adult help you find some seeds. You can bury the seeds in soil outside, or a small pot of dirt that you can keep indoors. As you cover the seed with dirt, think about how the disciples felt when they buried Jesus.

Soon you'll see sprouts poking through the soil! This reminds us how Jesus did not stay in the tomb, but rose to life again. Make sure to water your plant just enough to help it grow!
How is taking care of your plant similar to living life God's way? What instructions did Jesus give the disciples after the resurrection?

<u>My Time With God:</u>

The First Church

The Scripture: Acts 2:42-47

The book of Acts is about what happens after Jesus returns to heaven. We have a chance to see what the very first church was like. The apostles (the former disciples) taught the people. God's people learned together, worshiped together, prayed together, and at meals together. There were miracles, called signs and wonders! The people of the church shared everything they had.

Using these scriptures and your imagination, can you describe church for these Christians? How is it the same or different from our church today?

After Jesus rose from the dead and returned to heaven, He told the disciples to tell everyone about God and teach them to be followers of Jesus, too. The disciples were leaders of the early church. As the church grew, they needed more leaders. But, it was important to choose new leaders wisely for such a big job.

Our churches now have leaders, too. Who leads your church? What do they do?

Leadership is hard work! There are many things to do, like teaching, singing, fixing broken things, organizing service projects, and more. Also, church leaders pray and care for other church members, study God's word, and do their best to follow God's commands. We should take time to pray for our church leaders as they serve God and care for us.

You are growing up to be a leader, too. What would you like to do as a church leader some day? You don't have to wait until you're an adult to be part of a church community. What can you start learning now as you grow in faith?

Look up this memory verse and say it out loud: Hebrews 13:17 "Have confidence in your leaders and submit to their authority, because they keep watch over you."

Pray about it: Thank God for giving us good leaders. Ask Him to keep guiding our leaders and to help us grow into good leaders, too.

Active time!
Be a journalist! Interview a leader at your church or school. Ask them how they became a leader, what they like about their job, and what is difficult. Report your findings back to a friend or family member like a television broadcast or newspaper article.

Bonus fun: How would you like to be a leader? Are you good at showing other people how to do something by example? Are you more of a behind-the-scenes helper, ready to work hard at a job? There are many ways to be a leader, and we grow one step at a time. Think of a project you can help lead. Ask a parent or teacher for help if you need ideas. Then do something this week to start being a leader for the Lord.

My Time With God:

Saul's Conversion

The Scripture: Acts 9:1-19

Saul was not a very nice guy. He made life very difficult and dangerous for people who followed Jesus. Most of the Christians were afraid of him. One day, everything changed. When Saul was traveling down the road, and bright light suddenly shown down on him! A voice from heaven said, "Saul, why are you persecuting me?" That means the Lord was asking why Saul treated the Christians so badly. Then the Lord said, "I am Jesus! Now go to the city and I will tell you what to do there." Then Saul realized that he couldn't see anything anymore. But he went to the city like Jesus told him to do.

Ananias was a man who followed Jesus. He had heard about all the terrible things Saul had done. When he was praying that day, God told him to help Saul. How do you think Ananias felt when God told him to go see Saul?

Ananias trusted and believed God when He said Ananias would be safe. He followed God's instructions and discovered everything the way He said it would be. When Ananias met Saul and prayed for him, Saul could see again!

God changed Saul's heart. The change was so big that Saul had a new name- now he was Paul. Paul was learning to follow Jesus, too. Soon, he would travel all over the land to tell people about Jesus and help them follow Him, too.

Is there anyone you know that doesn't treat others very nicely? Is there a bully at school who is a little bit intimidating? God loves that person, too. In fact, God has a plan for his or her life, just like God had big plans for Paul!

Look up this memory verse and say it out loud: Acts 9:3-4 "Suddenly a light from heaven flashed around him. He fell to the ground. He heard a voice speak to him, 'Saul! Saul!' the voice said, 'Why are you persecuting me?'"

Pray about it: Thank God for loving us no matter how we behave. Ask God to help you see people through His eyes.

Active time!
It's not easy to depend on other people, but Saul needed lots of help while he was blind. Find a parent or buddy you trust, then cover your eyes with a blindfold. Let them help you walk, eat, and do other tasks. What is it like to need help? How do you think God was teaching Saul to depend on Him, too?

Bonus fun: God made a big change in Saul's heart. Have you heard of upcycling? It's changing something old into something new and better. For example, if you decorate an old can, you are able to use it as a beautiful pencil holder. What can you upcycle today? Ask a parent for ideas and help with any difficult projects.

My Time With God:

Dorcas

The Scripture: Acts 9:36-42

There were many women who followed God in the early church. They helped the poor, led house churches, learned from teachers like Peter and Paul, and served God in many other ways. One disciple was named Dorcas, but people also called her Tabitha.

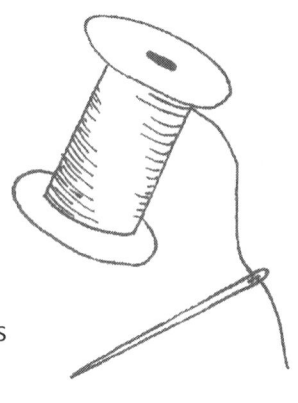

Dorcas was really good at making clothes. She loved to serve God and help others, so she made things for people in need. It meant a lot to the people to have these made especially for them. Dorcas also got to be part of one of God's miracles. She got sick and died, and everyone was sad. Then Peter came to visit. He went to the room where Dorcas was, and he prayed. God brought her back to life again!

What do you think it was like for her to be raised from the dead? Can you remember any other stories of people in the Bible who were raised from the dead?

When Dorcas made clothes, she didn't do it because she wanted everyone to know how good she was at sewing. She wanted the people to know that God loved them and would take care of them. After she was raised from the dead, Dorcas wanted everyone to know about God's great power. In everything she did, Dorcas helped people believe in God.

Look up this memory verse and say it out loud: Colossians 3:17 "And whatever you do, whether in word or deed, do it all in the name of the Lord Jesus, giving thanks to God the Father through him."

Pray about it: Thank God and give Him praise. Ask God for opportunities to help people believe in Him.

Active time!
Dorcas was known for her sewing abilities. Can you knit, cross-stich, or crochet? If you know someone who can do these or sew, ask them to teach you to make something simple. You can also get a how-to book from the library or craft store. You may be surprised at how much you love your new hobby!

Bonus fun: Do you know anyone who is sick? If so, make them a get-well card or care package. If everyone you know is healthy right now, ask a parent if there is someone in your church, school, or community that could use a little cheer while they are healing. What kind of things might help them feel better?

<u>**My Time With God:**</u>

Paul's Letters

The Scripture: Romans 12:1–8, Ephesians 1:3–10

After Saul changed his name to Paul, he started traveling and preaching. When he was away, he wrote letters to the people in many places who believed in Jesus. In his letter to the Christians in Rome, Paul shared ways God wants us to live our lives. Let's look at the things mentioned in this part of the letter:

Our bodies are a gift from God and we should take care of them.

Be careful not to do things just because everyone in the world is doing them. Not everybody follows Jesus, and they could be making bad decisions. Instead, learn God's ways and do them, even if it's not what everyone else is doing.

God gave everyone (including you) special gifts and talents. God made everyone (including you) different and unique for a very good reason. God has special things for everyone (including you) to do. But everyone (yup, including you!) has to make the choice to do these things to serve God.

So what do you think of this letter from Paul? Do you think these are things we should be doing?

The book of Ephesians is Paul's letter to the Christians in a place called Ephesus. The first thing he does is praise God. It's important to remember to thank and praise God before anything else. Next, Paul reminds us that God blesses us. That's a pretty big deal. Not only does God bless us, but God chose to bless us before the world was even made! Can you imagine that? Before God began to make the sun, the moon, the ocean, or the mountains, God decided to bless us. God loves us that much!

God didn't only want to bless us. He planned for us to be His children. That means that, just like a parent, God cares for us for our entire lives. Because He loves us so much, we are forgiven of our sins. Part of God's plan for us is to live with Him in heaven forever!

The words in Paul's letter can be difficult to understand, but it's important to take time to think about it and work through it. We need to know that God's love is so big that He planned good things for our lives before we were even born.

Look up this memory verse and say it out loud: Romans 12:5 "Though we are many, in Christ we form one body, and each member belongs to all the others."

Pray about it: Thank God for planning blessings for your life. Ask God to show you His plan and purpose for your future!

Active time!
Do you like to get mail? Share joy and send letters or a card to someone. You can tell them about what you're learning through your Bible time, draw a picture, or simply tell them about your

day and ask how they are doing. You could even send a few jokes that make you laugh or write them a poem. Think about the joy the Christians had when they got mail from Paul with the good news about Jesus.

Bonus fun: In our Ephesians scripture, Paul talked about God's plan for us. Ask your parents to show you baby books or photo albums with your baby pictures. How do you think your family planned for your arrival? Ask Mom or Dad to share the things they did to get ready for you to be born, as well as what they imagined you'd be like as you grew. How is God's plan for us like a parent's plan for a new baby? How is it different?

<u>My Time With God:</u>

Paul's Journey

The Scripture: Acts 17:22–28; 20:7-12

Paul traveled to many places to tell people the good news about Jesus. In this scripture, Paul has traveled to Greece. He tells the people in Athens- a city in Greece- about God. The people in Athens didn't know about God, but they believed in many different make-believe gods and built temples for them. But Paul told the people all about the one true God. He told them that God was bigger than any man-made temple, and that God made all the people! Paul also told them that they were God's children.

Have you ever told anyone about God? If you were talking to someone who didn't know anything about God, what would you tell them?

Another time, Paul visited a place called Troas. While he was there, he met with people in an upstairs room of a house. He was preaching and teaching for so long that a boy fell asleep- and fell out a window! But God healed the boy, and all the people were amazed at the miracle. What an adventure for Paul, the people, and especially the boy name Eutychus!

Look up this memory verse and say it out loud: Acts 17:24 "The God who made the world and everything in it is the Lord of heaven and earth and does not live in temples built by human hands."

Pray about it: Praise God for how wonderful He is. Ask God to help you tell others about Him.

Active time!
Many people like to make scrapbooks to help them remember their travels. Create a scrapbook for Paul that would help him remember the many places he has been. You can draw "photos", write captions, and use your imagination. Check out Acts 16:16-40 and Acts 28:1-10 for more places Paul visited and find out what happened there.

Bonus fun: Create a play or musical about Paul's journeys. You can gather your friends or family to play different parts, or do a one-person show where you play different characters or tell the story like Paul. Use props, costumes, and maybe even make scenery! Read more of the book of Acts to discover Paul's many adventures.

My Time With God:

Running the Race

The Scripture: 1 Corinthians 9:24-25

Paul wrote a letter to the people in a place called Corinth to tell them many things about following God and how much God loved them. Sometimes, it's hard to follow Jesus. Making good choices and listening to God's Word can be challenging. Paul wanted to encourage the Corinthians, so he started talking about something they knew- running races.

Have you ever run a race? Do you run laps during gym class? You probably know it takes hard work and focus to run a long distance. You must practice in order to get stronger. And you can't give up when you are tired; you have to keep going to reach the finish- even if you don't feel like it.

Living God's way can be like that, too. We have to practice making wise, godly choices. When we do, we get stronger and it becomes easier to make those choices. If we ever get tired of following God, we can't stop! We have to keep going every day. And just like finishing a race, there's a prize at the end. Once our life on earth is finished, we get a great reward in Heaven with God!

Look up this memory verse and say it out loud: 2 Timothy 4:7 "I have fought the good fight, I have finished the race, I have kept the faith."

Pray about it: Thank God for giving us new ways to understand Him. Ask God to help you keep choosing Him, even when you get tired or have a bad day.

Active time!
The best way to understand what Paul says about running a race is to practice running! How far can you go? How fast can you run? Find a buddy and run a race together. Where should your eyes look when you are running? How do you feel when the race is over? How is our life with Christ like running a race? For fun, if you have a race track for toy cars, you can race them, too!

Bonus fun: Find a buddy and play catch or soccer. These are games that go back and forth. They remind us that we never have to "run our race" by ourselves. God is always with us! We can talk to Him and listen to His Word all the time. The Lord is always right beside us, showing us how to make wise choices and helping us to love Him.

My Time With God:

What Is Sin?

The Scripture: Romans 3:23; James 4:17; 1 John 1:7-9

In Paul's letters, he often talked about something called sin. Sin means "to miss the mark", or make a mistake. Imagine that you are trying to shoot an arrow at a target. You aim, but you miss the middle and the arrow goes flying away. This is kind of like sin- we try to follow God's way, but sometimes we mess up and make poor choices that do not please God. In Romans, Paul tells us that we all have sinned- every single one of us.

Be honest- how have you sinned today? This week? This month? If you think you have been perfect, think again!

The good news is that our story doesn't end with sin. Because Jesus died on the cross, He took the punishment for all our mistakes, even the ones we haven't made yet. What good news!

The disciple John wrote letters, too, many years after Jesus returned to heaven. In one letter, he helps us remember the joy we have, even though we are sinners. He reminds us of what to do when we do make a bad decision and sin. First, we confess to God what we did wrong. Then, we ask for forgiveness. The Bible says that God will always forgive us, so we can say a happy thank you to the Lord!

Look up this memory verse and say it out loud: 1 John 1:9 "If we confess our sins, he is faithful and just and will forgive us our sins and purify us from all unrighteousness."

Pray about it: Tell God the ways you have sinned. Ask Him for forgiveness, then say a prayer of thanks to the Lord for His unfailing love.

Active time!
The word "sin" means "missing the mark." Create a toss game where you throw something at or into a target. You can also go outside and play basketball. Notice how it takes practice to hit your mark. It also takes practice for us to do the right thing and follow God's way. Share your game with someone and tell them what you've learned about sin.

Bonus fun: When you thought about your sins, was there anything you did that might've hurt someone you love? Did you fight with a sibling? Lie to your parents? Disobey? Call someone names at school? After you pray and ask God for forgiveness, write a note to the person you hurt when you sinned. Tell them you are sorry and ask for their forgiveness, too. Finally, tell them how much God loves them.

<u>My Time With God:</u>

Draw Close to God

The Scripture: James 4:7-8

Did you know that Jesus had brothers and sisters? One of His brothers, James, truly believed in Jesus after He died and was raised from the dead. James became another teacher and wrote letters like Paul, John, and the other apostles. The whole book of James is a letter to the people of God. In it, James tells people how to live a life that follows Christ.

Do you ever wonder how to be close to God? James says it is simple. Just draw close to God, and He will draw close to you. That means that spending time with the Lord will make you closer and closer to Him every day. You can do that by reading the Bible, praying, singing worship songs, or just being still and listening. Reading this book and doing the activities is another good way to spend time with God. So is memorizing scripture!

There were many people in the Bible who practiced what James is teaching. Moses would go up to a special mountain to spend time with God. David wrote songs of praise and even sad songs asking God to help. Jesus' friend, Mary, spent her time at His feet, listening to Him. Who else can you think of that stayed close to God?

Think back to the day you started this book. Do you feel any closer to Him now than you did that day? What can you do today to draw close to God?

Look up this memory verse and say it out loud: James 4:8 "Draw close to God, and He will draw close to you."
Pray about it: Thank God for being close to you. Ask Him to draw close to you all week long.

Active time!
Find some magnets and play with them. How do they stick to each other? Can you get them to push each other away? Look up how magnets work in a book or on the internet. For extra creativity, write the memory verse on a piece of paper or cardboard. Then, glue a magnet to the back and place it on the refrigerator where you will see it often.

Bonus fun: If we want strong friendships, we have to spend time with our friends. And if we want to have a strong friendship with God, we have to spend time with Him. Invite a friend over for a play date. Have fun with your friend and know that you are making your friendship strong by spending time together. Later, spend time with God and make your friendship with Him strong, too.

My Time With God:

Jesus Will Come Again

The Scripture: Revelation 4, 22:1-5; Isaiah 65:17-19

We know that, according to Jeremiah 29:11, God has good plans for us. God is thinking about the big picture! The scriptures we read today mention a few things about our long-term future. What do you think about what Isaiah says in this passage?

God gave a special vision to John, who wrote it down for us to read in what's now the book of Revelation. The descriptions are pretty amazing- beautiful pictures we can imagine. There will be a throne, a rainbow, and lots of light! There will be angels and praising there! What else do you find in John words about heaven in Revelation?

We think about God's glory as we look forward to heaven. The book of Revelation is full of colorful images, but there is something special about the verses we read today. They tell us how God will be the source of life there. The river that flows from God's throne gives life to the trees that grow. Also, God will be so bright that no one will need any other light- not even the sun!

But we don't have to wait for our future in heaven to see that we need God for life here on earth. We know that God made the sun that gives us light and the water that keeps us healthy. God keeps us safe and heals us when we are sick. What other ways do we need God for life?

Look up this memory verse and say it out loud: Revelation 22:5 "They will not need the light of a lamp or the light of the sun, for the Lord God will give them light."

Pray about it: Thank God for being our source of life and everything we need! Ask Him to help you remember to have hope because of His promises. Then, thank God for loving us so much that He prepared a beautiful eternity. Ask Him to keep giving you hope for the future.

Active time!
Using the descriptions of heaven in the Bible, create a piece of art that shows what you imagine heaven might be like. You don't have to limit yourself to only paper and marker or crayon. What other materials can you use to help illustrate what heaven might be like? Can you make your piece three-dimensional?

Bonus fun: When you're riding in the car this week, can you see where God is working? What things can you see that God has made? Which of these things do we need? Maybe it's the sunshine, or maybe it's helpful neighbors. What else can you see? Point these out to whoever else is with you (or see who can discover the most different things). Have fun!

My Time With God:

Are You a Writer Today? - A Do-It-Yourself Bible Time

Choose one or more of these topics and spend time journaling with God.

1. **Thank you, God!** : Find or remember a verse about thankfulness, and write it at the top of the page. Then, make a list of as many things as you can that make you feel thankful. Say a prayer to tell God how you feel.

2. **Nature reflection:** Find a chair by the window, look, and describe everything you can see with as many details as possible. How do you feel when you are surrounded by God's creation? What does nature remind you about God? For example, do tall trees make you think of how big God is? Or are rocks strong like Him? If you feel creative, write a poem or song about what you're thinking.

3. **God, I have a problem...:** Sometimes it's good to get away from the noise of our everyday life and take a break. This is also a good time to talk to God about things that are on our minds. Good things, bad things, big thing, small things (one thing two things red things blue things? Oh wait, that's Dr. Seuss....)- everything important to you is important to God. Write a letter to God about what's on your heart, including questions you have for Him.

4. **Story time:** Grab a Bible and find a story. Any story is good, even if it's one you know well or one that's brand new to you.

First, read the story. Ask God to show you what He wants you to see. Then, write the story from the point of view of one of the characters. Be creative! Imagine what it was like to be there- what your characters saw, felt, heard, or smelled.

5. **Any other journal ideas?** Write them!

Look up this memory verse and say it out loud: Psalm 19:14 "May these words of my mouth and this meditation of my heart be pleasing in your sight, Lord, my Rock and my Redeemer."

Pray about it: Thank God for giving us the gift of writing. Ask God to inspire the words on your page.

My Time With God:

Cardboard Box - A Do-It-Yourself Bible Time

Step 1: Find a cardboard box of any size.

Step 2: Choose your favorite Bible story.

Step 3: Creatively turn your box into a way to remember the story! Here are some ideas to help you begin:

1. **A shadow box** : Turn the box on its side and build a scene from your story inside- kind of like setting a play on a stage.

2. **A pedestal:** Turn your box upside down and use it as a base for a sculpture or an artifact from your story.

3. **A gift**: Create a gift for someone that helps share your story with them. You can wrap it and give it, or even mail it!

4. **A piece of your story:** Transform your box into an item from your story- a mountain, a chariot, a Book of the Law- use your imagination! You might even take your box apart and change the shape.

5. **A story cube:** Draw the story, scene by scene, on different sides of the box.

How else can you use your box to remember your favorite story?

Look up this memory verse and say it out loud: Psalm 92:5
"How great are your works, Lord, how profound your thoughts!"

Pray about it: Thank God for giving us the gift of imagination and creating. Ask God to inspire the work you do.

My Time With God:

Bible Time For a Friend - A Do-It-Yourself Bible Time

Now that you've worked your way through so many Bible Time activities, it's your turn to create one and share it with a friend!

1. **Choose a story** : Find it in the Bible, and write the scripture here:

2. **Why is it important?** Tell your friend what makes this story special to you. Write about the things you learned from it:

3. **Pick your favorite verse to learn**: You can save a verse from your story, or find another one that is important to you. This is a good verse to memorize so you can keep it with you always. Write it here:

4. **The activity:** Here's the fun part! Find an activity that helps you think about and remember your story. You can use one of your favorites from this book or design your own. Explain it:

5. **The prayer:** This is the most important part. Write a short prayer for you and your friend to say together:

Have fun sharing the joy of Bible Time!

My Time With God:

Serving God - A Do-It-Yourself Bible Time

The Scripture: 1 Peter 4:10-11

There are many places in the Bible that instruct us to serve God by helping others. Can you think of any verses besides what you just read? Write them here:

Have you ever been part of a service project before? Have you helped others in some way? Remember it here:

Are there people you think about that you want to help? If you could do anything in the world to help someone, what would it be?

Look up this memory verse and say it out loud: 1 Peter 4:10
"Each of you should use whatever gift you have received to serve others, as faithful stewards of God's grace in its various forms."

Pray about it: Thank God for giving us clear instructions on how to follow His commands. Ask God to help you find ways to serve Him by helping others.

Active time!
Pray, think, and design your own project that serves God by serving others. Asking an adult for help is a good way to make it happen!

My Time With God:

Wrapping Up This Bible Time

Whew! You just completed a lot of quality time with the Lord! You did a great job sticking with it and making it to the end of this book. God loves to spend time with His children, and He had a great time with you as you read, learned, prayed, grew, played, and used your imagination. He created you to do all those things!

Before you turn the last page and close this book, decide what you will do next. Now you know how to create your own Bible Time activities. How will you continue to pray and play to grow closer to the Lord? Write your plan here:

"Rejoice always, pray continually, give thanks in all circumstances; for this is God's will for you in Christ Jesus."   *1 Thess. 5:16-18*

ACKNOWLEDGMENTS

Many thanks to the wonderful people who helped bring *Bible Time for Active Kids* to life: JJ, the Snyder family, the Lie family, Melissa, Lara, and Dallas. All thanks, glory, and praise to God our Father and the Lord Jesus Christ!

ABOUT THE AUTHOR

Malinda Fugate grew up in children's ministry from the moment her pastor father plopped her down into the church nursery full of crayons and donated Fisher Price toys. Since then, it's been a non-stop whirlwind of flannel board, VBS, and hand-motioned songs. After two decades of dedicated volunteer service, she now serves full time as the Children's Education Director at Faith Presbyterian Church in Rolling Hills, California.

Malinda earned a communications degree with a theatre emphasis from Azusa Pacific University, then worked behind the scenes at the Los Angeles Salem radio stations, including The Fish and KKLA. Her other writing includes commercial copywriting, various faith-based stage plays, and *The Pen and The Sword: Connecting with the Word of God*, a creative writing journal for kids. She lives by the beach with her two pups, Yoshi and Poseidon.

Manufactured by Amazon.ca
Bolton, ON